William McKinley: The Life and Legacy of the Third President to Be Assassinated

By Charles River Editors

About Charles River Editors

Charles River Editors provides superior editing and original writing services across the digital publishing industry, with the expertise to create digital content for publishers across a vast range of subject matter. In addition to providing original digital content for third party publishers, we also republish civilization's greatest literary works, bringing them to new generations of readers via ebooks.

Sign up here to receive updates about free books as we publish them, and visit Our Kindle Author Page to browse today's free promotions and our most recently published Kindle titles.

Introduction

"That's all a man can hope for during his lifetime - to set an example - and when he is dead, to be an inspiration for history." – William McKinley

Although he is often overlooked in American history today, few presidents marked a turning point for the country quite like William McKinley. As the last president to have served in the Civil War, he represented the end of an era, while at the same time his pro-business policies set in motion the Progressive Era, a period almost universally associated with Theodore Roosevelt.

Of course, the reason that period is aligned with Roosevelt is because McKinley had the unfortunate distinction of being one of only four presidents to be assassinated. In September 1901, the city of Buffalo was full of celebration. The Pan-American Exposition was ongoing, and it brought notable figures to northern New York, including President McKinley, who had been reelected less than a year earlier. But also in Buffalo was Leon Czolgosz, a young man who had turned to anarchy years earlier after losing his job, Embracing his philosophy wholeheartedly, Czolgosz believed it was his mission to take down a powerful leader he considered oppressive, and McKinley's attendance gave him the chance.

President James Garfield had been assassinated just 20 years earlier, but McKinley didn't worry about presidential security or his own safety, and that was the case in Buffalo. McKinley's insistence on greeting the public and shaking hands allowed Czolgosz to walk up to him on September 6, 1901 at a public reception in the Temple of Music on the expo grounds and shoot him point blank, with one bullet grazing the president and another lodging in his abdomen. In the aftermath of the shooting, as Czolgosz was beaten and seized by the crowd, he uttered, "I done my duty." For his part, McKinley said, "He didn't know, poor fellow, what he was doing. He couldn't have known."

Despite being president, McKinley's medical services were shoddy, and given the still primitive medical standards of the early 20th century, gunshots to the abdomen often brought death. One of the best known aspects of the assassination is that Thomas Edison's x-ray machine was on hand and may have been used to try to locate the bullet that doctors couldn't find, but for reasons that remain unknown, the x-ray machine was not used.

Nevertheless, McKinley seemed to improve over the next few days, and people became optimistic he would be all right. As H. Wayne Morgan, one of McKinley's biographers, noted, "His hearty constitution, everyone said, would see him through. The doctors seemed hopeful, even confident... It is difficult to understand the cheer with which they viewed their patient. He was nearly sixty years old, overweight, and the wound itself had not been thoroughly cleaned or traced. Precautions against infections, admittedly difficult in 1901, were negligently handled." Ultimately, McKinley's wounds became gangrenous a week after he was shot, and after he took a turn for the worse, he died on the morning of September 14, nearly 8 days after he was shot.

McKinley was the third president to be assassinated, and today he is often remembered as one of the presidents to die in office after being elected every 20 years after William Henry Harrison's 1840 election through John F. Kennedy's 1960 election. However, the most notable consequence of the assassination is who it brought to power. Ironically, New York Governor Theodore Roosevelt's political enemies hoped to rid the state of their progressive governor by elevating him to national prominence. At the Republican National Convention in Philadelphia, the New York machine leaders decided to promote Roosevelt for the vice presidency, and in so doing, remove him from New York. At the time, the vice president was notoriously insignificant in national politics, so the political machinists thought that making Roosevelt the vice president would turn him into a nobody.

Initially, they encountered a problem when McKinley's campaign chief, Mark Hanna, did not think Roosevelt would make a good addition to the Republican ticket. In time, however, they managed to convince Hanna and most other delegates at the National Convention that Roosevelt was the perfect addition to the GOP ticket. Roosevelt was initially unsure of the position; while many thought it would end his political career, Roosevelt wasn't even sure that was a bad thing. Perhaps it was time to return to the countryside, anyway. As a result, after some convincing, Roosevelt accepted the nomination as Vice President alongside President McKinley, and the pair won the election of 1900, making Roosevelt the Vice President in March 1901.

William McKinley: The Life and Legacy of the Third President to Be Assassinated chronicles the life and death of the president. Along with pictures and a bibliography, you will learn about McKinley like never before.

McKinley's Early Years

William McKinley Jr. was born on January 29, 1843 in Niles, Ohio, the seventh child of William McKinley, Sr. and Nancy Allison McKinley. McKinley's early biographer Charles Olcott described his ancestry: "The early ancestors of William McKinley were Scottish Highlanders, a race of men distinguished for the strength with which they fought and overcame the hardships of their surroundings. Bred in the fastnesses of the Caledonian Mountains, where Nature offered little chance to earn a living and few of the comforts of life, these men struggled bravely to maintain their homes. The frequent encroachments upon their patrimony by greedy barons of the Lowlands were met with a fierce resistance, until the Highlanders became famous, not only as fighting men of the staunchest quality, but as patriots of the truest type, ready to lay down their lives at a moment's notice in defense of their homes, their families, and their native land."

The first McKinley to settle in the New World was David McKinley. In 1743, records show that he purchased 316 acres of land overlooking the Susquehanna River in York County, Pennsylvania. John McKinley, David's eldest son, was born around 1728, and he went on to become a large landholder in York county and served in the York County Militia during the Revolution.

David McKinley, the great-grandfather of William McKinley, was born May 16, 1755. During the Revolution, he served as a private in the militia, and after the war he moved to Mercer County, Pennsylvania, and then in 1814 to Columbiana County, Ohio. Of his 10 children, his second was James Stevenson McKinley, William McKinley's grandfather, born September 19, 1783. He married Mary Rose, and James became manager of a charcoal furnace at New Lisbon, Ohio. Their son, William McKinley Sr., was born November 15, 1807.

Octott described William McKinley, Sr.'s early life and career: "Like his father, he was a 'founder,' or manager of blast furnaces, a trade which in the pioneer days required a strong physique and skill of many and varied kinds...it is said that there were three books which he kept constantly at hand, and read for a few minutes at a time whenever he had an opportunity. These were the Bible, Shakespeare, and Dante. His first business venture on his own account was made in 1830, when as a partner in the firm of Campbell, McKinley & Dempsey, he rented a furnace at Niles, owned by James Heaton. Later he formed a partnership with his brother-in-law, Jacob Reep, buying or renting furnaces, first at Fairfield, then New Lisbon, and finally at Niles, Ohio. In 1829 he married Nancy Allison."

McKinley, Sr.

Nancy Allison McKinley, William, Jr.'s mother, was of Scottish decent. She was described by Olcott as "a woman of strong, rugged, positive character." Olcott explained, "Her sturdy Scotch disposition made her a thrifty housewife and a stern disciplinarian, though her children obeyed her wishes more from love than through fear. She expected obedience and received it. The family were neither rich nor poor. They lived simply, dressed as became their station, and commanded the respect of the community wherever they resided."

The house William grew up in was one befitting their station in their community. Olcott noted, "The house where he was born was a small frame cottage, standing on a corner of the main street in the village of Niles. The lower floor on the left side was used as a store. It was a humble home, presided over by a heroic mother, who managed by hard work and good sense to make the slender income of her husband meet the necessities of a large family. In this, both boys and girls were taught to help, and it may be surmised that the household tasks, though rigorously insisted upon, were never thought too irk some, for the children, without exception, loved their mother devotedly."

Along with his brothers and sisters, William attended school at Niles and engaged in activities typical of a boy his age. Olcott continued, "The martial spirit aroused by the Mexican War resulted in the formation of a company of small boys who drilled on Saturday afternoons and William was one of those who marched about proudly with paper cap and wooden sword." He and his family were members of the local Methodist Episcopal Church, where William attended Sunday School and worshiped with his family every Sunday.

When William reached age 9, his father decided to move his family to Poland, Ohio, a small village in Mahoning. William and his siblings enrolled in the local Poland Seminary, where McKinley, Sr.. was forced to remain in Niles to attend to his business, seeing his family only on the weekends. Henry Howe described Poland in 1847 as "one of the neatest villages in the State. The dwellings are usually painted white and have an air of comfort. Considerable business centers here from the surrounding country, which is fertile. In the vicinity is coal and iron of excellent quality...Poland contains 5 stores, 1 Presbyterian and 1 Methodist Church, an academy, an iron foundry, 1 grist, 1 saw, 1 oil, and 1 clothing mill and about 100 dwellings."

While at Poland Seminary, McKinley attended a Methodist revival camp meeting which left a profound impression on him. Olcott relayed a telling anecdote from the period: "At one of these camp-meetings, following the usual invitation from the minister for those who wished to 'profess conversion' to come forward to the 'mourner's bench,' William McKinley, Jr., ten years old, marched up the aisle with manly dignity and united with the church 'on probation.' On the same day his sister Sarah, two years older, took the same step. Each acted independently of the other and without urging from their mother. No doubt the good lady shed tears of joy abundantly at this answer to her prayers. She came to think of William as a candidate for the ministry and indulged the hope that one day he might become a bishop. His own ecclesiastical ambition was confined to the desire that he might sometime be a trustee of the church — a wish that was granted in due season. A higher ambition was to live the life of a true, earnest, and consistent Christian, and this William McKinley did to the day of his death."

McKinley at the age of 15

McKinley graduated from Poland Seminary in 1859 and enrolled the following year at Allegheny College, but Olcott pointed out that there was little of record during this time: "He remained only a short time and returned to Poland on account of illness. His intention was to go back to college after a brief rest. But it was a period of 'hard times' and his father's finances were in bad condition. Anna was teaching school and others of the family were at work, so William decided that in justice to the others he must at least earn the money for his future education. Teaching made the first appeal to him, and hearing of a vacancy in the Kerr District School he applied for the position. The salary was twenty five dollars a month and the teacher was expected to 'board around.' The school was two miles and a half from Poland. McKinley preferred to live at home, and therefore walked the distance, morning and evening, frequently leaping fences and crossing fields to save time. When school closed he took a position as clerk in the post-office at Poland."

McKinley's War Years

The firing on Fort Sumter in April 1861 heralded the beginning of the Civil War, and when it became clear that there would be no settlement with the seceded states, President Lincoln called for the states who remained in the Union to supply volunteers for what he (and everyone else) believed would be a short conflict. Across the North, young men full of patriotic enthusiasm formed new volunteer units in towns large and small, and Poland was no different. Olcott explained, "On a day in June, 1861, the sidewalks were filled with people, the horses, wagons, and buggies of hundreds of farmers lined the streets, and a little squad of soldiers, led by a veteran of the Mexican War, was marching up and down, to the shrill but inspiring notes of the fife and the noisy beating of drums. The balconies of the old Sparrow House (it had a double veranda then) were crowded with women, some singing, others crying. A tense nervous strain was felt by everyone. The leading lawyer of the vicinity, Charles E. Glidden, was making a speech from the front of the tavern. As the result of his eloquence, man after man stepped up to volunteer, and as they did so, the crowd cheered and women pinned red, white, and blue badges upon the new soldiers. Young men talked glibly of the glory of war and the fun of camp-life. Older men were more serious, but there was a contagion of enthusiasm so strong that Poland furnished its full complement of men as volunteers, and not a man was ever drafted from the village."

Now 18, William was no different and had a clear vision of his duty. Along with his cousin, William McKinley Osbourne, McKinley decided to enlist in the company from Poland, seeing it as his duty. He managed to overcome his mother's concerns, and he and his cousin ultimately enlisted in the Poland company at Camp Chase, near Columbus. The regiment was later mustered into the 23rd Ohio Volunteers, Company E. Each young man had signed up for three months, but when they reached Columbus they discovered that the quota of three month volunteers was full, meaning they would have to sign up for three years or return home. To a man, each enlisted for the three years.

In 1889, McKinley gave a speech before the Grand Army of the Republic, where he said of volunteer soldiers like himself: "They enlisted in the army with no expectation of promotion; not for the paltry pittance of pay; not for fame or popular applause, for their services, however efficient, were not to be heralded abroad. They entered the army moved by the highest and purest motives of patriotism, that no harm might befall the republic. We counted no cost when the war commenced. We knew little of the great sacrifices which were to come or the scope and extent of that great war; we only knew that the Union was threatened with overthrow; we only knew that the nation of our fathers was in danger by the hand of treason. And that alone made the liberty-loving people indifferent to cost and consequences, caring nothing but to smite the hand which would seize our priceless inheritance, and scorning all other considerations that they might preserve to mankind the best Government in. the world. It was then that the genius of self-government asserted itself, and the whole North was turned into a camp for muster and military instruction. The citizens voluntarily came together to join an army bound together in a common cause for common purpose – the preservation of the Union. It was an awful experience for the American boy, who knew nothing of war, in many instances, save as he had read of it in the glamour of history, and who in many cases had never so much as seen a company of armed men. Unused to hardships, unaccustomed to toil, undrilled in the tactics of war, with a mother's blessing and a father's affectionate farewell, he went forth with firm resolve to give up all, even the last drop of his life's blood, that this nation should be saved."

The first major of the 23rd Ohio was Rutherford B. Hayes, another future president, and unlike many of the other officers, Hayes quickly won the respect of his men. McKinley delivered a memorial address for Hayes in 1893, during which he said, "The first headquarters of the regiment were at Camp Chase. I had never seen Hayes until he reported to the regiment, and I recall our first meeting the better because of a little incident which happened when, with all the pride of new recruits, we came to receive our muskets. The State could furnish only the most inferior guns. These we positively and proudly refused to accept. We would accept nothing but the best. The officers spent most of the day trying to persuade us to receive the guns for a few weeks, if only for the purpose of drill. None of us knew how to use any kind of a musket at that time, but we thought we knew our rights and we were all conscious of our importance. They assured us that more modern guns would soon be supplied. Major Hayes did the talking to our company, and I shall that many of the most decisive battles of history had been won with the rudest weapons. At Lexington and Bunker Hill and many other engagements of the Revolution our forefathers had triumphed over the well-equipped English armies with the very poorest firearms — and that even pikes and scythes had done good work in that glorious conflict. Should we be less patriotic than our brave ancestors? Should we hesitate at the very start of another struggle for liberty and union, for the best and freest Government on the face of the earth, because we were not pleased with the pattern of our muskets, or with the caliber of our rifles? I cannot, at this late day, recall his exact words, but I shall never forget his warmth of patriotic feeling and the sound sense with which he appealed to us. That was our first and last mutiny. We accepted the old-fashioned guns, took what was offered us cheerfully, and Hayes held us captive from that hour. From that very moment he had our respect and admiration, which never weakened, but increased during the four eventful years that followed."

Hayes during the war

McKinley in 1865

The regiment was first ordered to Clarksburg, Virginia (now West Virginia), arriving on July 27, 1861. That was less than a week after the Confederate victory at the First Battle of Bull Run, an ominous indication that the war would take much longer than anyone envisioned. From there, the 23rd Ohio was moved to Weston. In a letter to a cousin written in early August 1861, McKinley recounted his early experiences in the Army: "Your letter dated the 6th inst. was received this morning and its contents perused with pleasure. Although it did not come to hand as early as expected, yet 'better late than never.' We are encamped at Weston, a small town in Western Virginia of about eight hundred inhabitants, and looks as if it might have once been a village of some stir and vitality, but since the war broke out it has buried all its vital parts in oblivion. Our regiment is scattered all over the State of Virginia. Five hundred of them are with the Seventh Regiment under Colonel Tyler now marching to Galley Bridge, one hundred on their way to Sutton, and others scattered here and there, all over the hills and valleys, of the 'Old Dominion State.' Three hundred of us remain here as a guard and I can tell you we are doing the thing up 'bravely,' yea 'heroicly.' We have entire possession of the town. The other night, some of the Twenty-third Regiment, while out on 'picket' some two or three miles from camp guarding a bridge en route for Sutton, and lying in ambush around it, returned in the morning possessed of quite a 'scary' story, which they related. The substance was as follows, that while out in the darkness of night, when all was calm and quiet as the sea on a still summer's day, a strange noise was heard about the above named bridge and on its roof was the pattering of stones, distinctly heard; this was a terrific, appalling report, and preparations were made to catch the rebels. On the following night, four of us volunteered to go out and catch the 'seceshers' if possible. Accordingly we started out about dusk led by a certain lieutenant of our regiment. It would have done you good to have seen the above lieutenant prodding the thick bushes with his gilded sword, fancying to himself that he saw the hideous monster in the shape of a rebel. Ah, the ambitious officer was disappointed; instead of sticking a secesh, he without doubt stuck a skunk. We came to this conclusion from the fact that a strong smell, a venomous smell, instantly issued from the bushes. We imagined a great many strange things to appear before us, but all proved to be shadows instead of realities. We at last arrived at the hitherto 'scary' spot, stationed ourselves, and it was my lot to be placed in a cornfield by the roadside. I stayed there until morning, cocked my old musket, and was almost in the act of shooting a number of times, when the strange vision would disappear and on examination I would discover a piece of fox-fire, an itinerant 'hog,' or a lost calf, which had undoubtedly wandered from its mother in its infantile days. We returned in the morning, sleepy, tired, and not as full of romance as the night before. Enough of this. We have a very nice place for encampment, on one of Virginia's delightful hills and surrounded by the Western Branch of the Monongahela River. We have some fine times bathing in the above river. We are under the strictest military discipline and nothing is allowed but what is guaranteed by the army regulations. Your kindness, Cousin William, is highly appreciated by me in offering me anything that I need; this tells me that I have a place in your affections and in answer would say that I would like papers as often as you can conveniently send them. We cannot get papers here but seldomly. As to post age stamps they are very hard to get, but think I will receive some in a few days, and as to money I have none, but can get along without it until Uncle Sam pays us off. When that will be I do not know. We may have to leave here very soon, but I think it hardly probable. I received a letter from Annie a few days since, and was glad to hear from her. I presume she will soon be with you from what she writes."

The monotony of military service ended for the 23rd Ohio on the evening of September 10, when the young boys experienced their first taste of battle at Carnifex Ferry., where they succeeded in driving the Confederate forces from the field. McKinley recalled, "This was our first real fight, and the effect of the victory was of far more consequence to us than the battle itself. It gave us confidence in ourselves and faith in our commander. We learned that we could fight and whip the rebels on their own ground."

Other than a few skirmishes and long marches, the 23rd Ohio did not participate in any major battles for almost a year, but that changed on September 17, 1862. The regiment had not been involved in the disastrous defeat at the Second Battle of Bull Run in late August 1862, but it was on hand for the Battle of Antietam, which remains the bloodiest day in American history. On September 17, 1862, Robert E. Lee's Confederate Army of Northern Virginia fought George McClellan's Union Army of the Potomac outside Sharpsburg along Antietam Creek, and that day, nearly 25,000 would become casualties and Lee's army would barely survive fighting the much bigger Northern army. Although the battle was tactically a draw, it resulted in forcing Lee's army out of Maryland and back into Virginia, making it a strategic victory for the North and an opportune time for President Abraham Lincoln to issue the Emancipation Proclamation, freeing all slaves in the rebellious states.

For those reasons, Antietam is remembered as one of the major turning points of the Civil War, but it is often overlooked that the bloody battle only represented the climactic culmination of a 3 week campaign that saw George McClellan cautiously pull a fragmented Union army together and begin tracking Lee's army into Maryland. Sizing up McClellan, Lee had split his army up during its invasion, including sending Stonewall Jackson's men to Harpers Ferry, but the whole course of the campaign and possibly the war changed when the Union Army somehow found a copy of Lee's marching orders, telling them where the Confederate army would be and when. To Lee's surprise, McClellan's army began advancing far more rapidly, including attacking them at South Mountain before cornering them along Antietam Creek outside of Sharpsburg.

McKinley graphically described the horrors he experienced during that battle: "It was a lovely September day — an ideal Sunday morning. McClellan's army, with Burnside's Corps in front, was passing up the mountain by the National Road. General Cox's Ohio Division led Burnside's Corps, and the Twenty-third Ohio was in the lead of that division. Hayes was ordered to take one of the mountain paths and move to the right of the rebels. At nine o'clock the rebel picket was driven back, and on our pushing forward the rebels advanced upon us in strong force. Our regiment was quickly formed in the woods and charged over rocks and broken ground, through deep under brush, under the heavy fire of the enemy at short range, and, after one of the hottest fights of the war, we drove them out of the woods and into an open field near the hilltop. Another charge was ordered by Hayes. No sooner had he given the word of command than a minie ball from the enemy shattered his left arm above the elbow, crushing the bone to fragments. He called to a soldier to tie his handkerchief about the wound, but turning faint he fell, his men passing over and beyond him into the fight, where he had ordered them. When he regained consciousness, Hayes found himself under a heavy fire, with the bullets pelting the ground all about him. He feared that his men were retreating, but he was soon reassured when, on calling out, he was carried in safety to friendly cover. Wounded and bleeding as he was, he was not wholly unconscious of what was going on about him, and ordered his men to hold their position, which they did under Major Comly, who, through the rest of the day, commanded the regiment with rare judgment and courage. The regiment made three successful charges in that fight, and lost nearly two hundred men — half of the effective force — in action."

At the time of the battle, McKinley served as commissary sergeant, and throughout the fighting that day he kept going to the front with wagons loaded with rations and hot coffee. Olcott wrote, "Heedless of shot and shell, he worked his way over rough ground and through mud-holes that all but stopped his progress, until at last, late in the afternoon, he reached the rear of his brigade and was greeted with a cheer, which so astonished the division commander at the front that he sent an aide to inquire the cause." Hayes would later say of McKinley's valor, "From his hands every man in the regiment was served with hot coffee and warm meats, a thing that had never occurred under similar circumstances in any other army in the world. He passed under fire and delivered, with his own hands, these things, so essential for the men for whom he was laboring." For his service, McKinley was promoted to second lieutenant of Company D on November 3, 1862.

A monument to McKinley on the Antietam battlefield

A plaque on the monument commemorating McKinley as a soldier and president

The 23rd Ohio next saw action in April 1864, when they took part in a raid on the Virginia and Tennessee Railroad. McKinley remembered, "It was a rough and trying march, over mountains and through deep ravines and dense woods, with snows and rains that would have checked the advance of any but the most determined. Daily we were brought in contact with the enemy. We penetrated a country where guerrillas were abundant and where it was not an unusual thing for our own men to be shot from the underbrush — murdered in cold blood."

The march culminated with the Battle of Cloyd's Mountain on May 9, 1864. With Robert E. Lee's Army of Northern Virginia continuing to frustrate the Union Army of the Potomac's attempts to take Richmond in 1862 and 1863, President Lincoln shook things up by turning command of all the armies of the United States to Ulysses S. Grant in March 1864. Lee had won stunning victories at battles like Chancellorsville and Second Bull Run by going on the offensive and taking the strategic initiative, but Grant and Lincoln had no intention of letting him do so anymore. Attaching himself to the Army of the Potomac, Grant ordered Army of the Potomac commander George Meade, "Lee's army is your objective point. Wherever Lee goes, there you will go also."

At the Battle of the Wilderness (May 5-7, 1864), Grant and Lee fought to a standstill in their first encounter, failing to dislodge each other despite incurring nearly 30,000 casualties between the Union Army of the Potomac and the Confederate Army of Northern Virginia. However, after the fierce fighting, Grant continued to push his battered but resilient army south.

Civil War fans and historians are generally familiar with the ensuing major battles that took place at Spotsylvania, the North Anna, Cold Harbor, and then the subsequent siege of Petersburg, but as the armies were moving towards Spotsylvania, Grant detached some forces in an effort to destroy railroads in western Virginia that the Confederates used to ship men and material to the Western Theater. With William Tecumseh Sherman's command attempting to take Atlanta from Joseph E. Johnston's Army of Tennessee, it was crucial to hamper the Confederacy's ability to reinforce itself in either direction.

Eventually, Union and Confederate forces met each other at the Battle of Cloyd's Mountain, resulting in one of the most savage battles of the war. There were over 1,000 combined casualties at the battle, resulting in the Union losing 10% of its total men in the battle and the Confederates losing an astounding 20%. The battle, a short but intense engagement, ended with a Union victory that allowed them to sever the last railroad lines connecting Virginia and Tennessee, which meant to a large degree that the Eastern Theater and Western Theater were divided for the Confederacy.

During that battle, the 23rd Ohio was ordered to charge the Confederate positions, which consisted of reinforced earthworks on the first crest of the mountain. McKinley recalled, "The hill itself was thickly wooded, steep and difficult of access, and was skirted by a stream of water two or three feet deep. The approach was through a beautiful meadow five or six hundred yards in width. At the word of command the regiment advanced at double-quick across the meadow, under a very heavy fire of musketry and artillery, to the foot of the mountain, across the stream. The regiment advanced steadily to this point, without returning the fire of the enemy; and, after a short pause, a furious assault was made upon the enemy's works, carrying them and capturing two pieces of artillery... The enemy fell back to the second crest or ridge of the mountain, where a determined attempt was made to form a line, but, after a short struggle, he was driven from there in full retreat. Reinforcements arriving on the field, a third attempt was made to make a stand, but unsuccessfully. The struggle at the guns was of the fiercest description. The rebel artillery men attempted to reload their pieces when our line was not more than ten paces distant."

At a reunion for the regiment in 1877, McKinley simply said of Cloyd's Mountain, "The Battle of Cloyd Mountain, under General Crook, famous in the regiment's history, must command a passing word. Skillful and furious, it tried the mettle of the best men."

George Crook, commander of Union forces at Cloyd's Mountain

Over the next few weeks, the 23rd Ohio marched through western Virginia, reaching Charleston, West Virginia on July 1, 1864. From there, they were ordered into the Shenandoah Valley to help stop the raids of Confederate General Jubal Early into Maryland and Pennsylvania. By September 19, 1864.the regiment, as part of the forces under General Philip H. Sheridan, fought in the Battle of Opequon near Winchester. The regiment also participated in the fighting at Fisher's Hill and Cedar Creek. For his "gallant and meritorious service," McKinley was promoted to brevet major of volunteers by President Lincoln on March 13, 1865. Olcott noted, "When the war came to an end, McKinley found himself at twenty-two a major with four years of valuable experience and an enviable record. There was strong temptation to take a permanent position in the regular army. He had entered the service a frail youth of eighteen. He came out a mature man, of vigorous health and bodily strength. He would have made an excellent army officer. But other considerations, including, no doubt, the wishes of his mother, prevailed, and on July 26, 1865, he was mustered out. At the present writing only two of the old Poland Company are still living. In talking with one of these veterans I asked what he thought of McKinley as a soldier. 'Why,' he replied simply, 'he did just what the rest of us did. Never shirked his duty. He was a good square fellow.' No better compliment could have been paid."

McKinley later reflected on what the war experience meant to himself and the millions of soldiers who had fought for the Union: "My friends, we had a million soldiers in the field when the war terminated, and the highest testimony to their character is found in the fact that when the muster-out came, and that vast army, which for years had been accustomed to war and carnage, returned to their homes, they dropped into the quiet walks of citizenship, and no trace of them was ever discernible except in their integrity of character, their intense patriotism, and their participation in the growth and development and maintenance of the Government which they had contributed so much to save."

The Start of McKinley's Political Career

After the war, McKinley decided he wanted to practice law, and he began studying under fellow Civil War veteran Charles E. Glidden, a lawyer who practiced in Poland. After a year, he enrolled at Albany Law School in New York. His roommate, George F. Arrell, later discussed their time at the school with Olcott: "'Those days are a lovely memory. McKinley,' he said, 'was a delightful companion. He was jolly, always good-natured, and looked at the bright side of everything. He was a sociable fellow, liked the theater, and was fond of good company. He did not indulge in sport of any kind, but in those days a man could go through college without doing so. He was thoroughly genuine, chaste in every way, and despised vulgarity. He never quarreled, but he had a mind of his own and was very determined. Even at that time he had made up his mind to enter public life, and clearly showed an ambition to go to Congress. He worked very hard, often reading until one or two o'clock in the morning. It was his very great industry, rather than genius, that paved the way for his success.'"

McKinley did not finish the course before he moved back to Ohio in 1867, but he was still admitted to the bar in Warren, and he later moved to Canton. In Canton, where his sister Anna was teaching school, he opened his law office, and over the coming year he formed a partnership with a more experienced lawyer and former judge named George W. Belden. His reputation as a lawyer grew and brought him a level of financial success that allowed him to buy a block of buildings on Main Street that he rented out. Justice William R, Day later spoke of McKinley's qualities as a lawyer: "In the trial of a case Major McKinley gained the confidence of the jury by the fairness and courtesy of his conduct, and into all his arguments was thrown the silent but potent influence of a character beyond reproach. To the court, he was thorough and logical, and always fair; to a jury, he had the same power of epigrammatic expression which has enabled him to state party policies and political views in phrases which compass a great truth in a few plain words. He had the faculty of putting things so that the jury could readily comprehend and follow his arguments. He spoke to them as he has since spoken to the people, appealed to their judgment and understanding, rather than to passion or prejudice."

The Stark County Bar Association, in a memorial they issued upon McKinley's death, said of him, "His career at the bar gave ample evidence of that greatness of mind, purity of character, and kindness of heart, now known of all men, and of which his future career gave so many and striking illustrations. To every cause he gave a full measure of preparation. He was particularly distinguished as an advocate, presenting his cause to juries in such fair and just manner as to command their confidence and respect. To the court, upon questions of law, he was lucid, strong, and convincing, never pressing an argument which he did not believe in himself. To his adversaries, at the trial table, he was ever courteous and considerate, realizing that the objects of legal investigation are to arrive at the truth and sub serve the ends of justice. He always aimed to keep forensic discussion upon the high plane of honest difference as to law or fact, and never indulged in personalities with opposite counsel or witnesses. To his colleagues he was ever kind and considerate, always doing his share of the labor in a case, and never shirking responsibility or withholding from his associate the share of honor and praise which was his due."

Shortly after he began his legal career, McKinley took his first tentative steps into the world of politics. When his former commanding officer and fiend, Rutherford B. Hayes, ran for governor in 1867, McKinley spoke on his behalf in Stark County. Having impressed the local Republican Party, in 1869 the Republicans nominated McKinley for the post of county prosecutor, and he was elected to the post despite the fact it was in a heavily Democratic county. In 1871, he lost reelection to the post by a mere 143 votes.

The sting of his first political loss was softened by events in McKinley's personal life. In 1870, McKinley met and began to court Ida Saxton, the daughter of prominent Canton businessman James A. Saxton. Olcott provided the details of the young lawyer's proposal: "The circumstances of the proposal were revealed, so far as they need be in such a matter, by Major McKinley himself. He was returning by carriage, to Canton from Massillon, in 1895, under escort of some of his fellow townsmen, during the closing days of an arduous political campaign. As they reached a certain hill in the outskirts of the town, the governor remarked, reminiscently, 'This, gentlemen, is where my fate was settled.' He then told the story of how he once drove up that hill with 'Ida,' behind a team of bay horses, how diffident he felt about broaching the subject that was uppermost in his mind, how he formed a resolution to know his fate, then and there, and how happy he felt, when, upon reaching a certain red brick house at the top of the hill, he received the answer for which his heart had yearned."

Ida McKinley

They were married on January 25, 1871 in the First Presbyterian Church of Canton, and after honeymooning in New York City, they returned to Canton. On Christmas Day that year, their daughter Katherine was born. Katherine was joined by a sister, Ida, in 1873, but the infant died a few months later, and little Katherine died of typhoid fever in 1875. McKinley's wife never recovered from the loss of her children. Olcott explained, "This final blow, falling upon a mind and body already staggering beneath a burden of sorrow too heavy to carry, came near ending the mother's life. But strong arms were ready to catch her as she fell. Infinite patience was there to nurse her back to life. The devoted husband rallied to meet the emergency, and, though himself oppressed by grief and a sense of bitter disappointment, he was able, in time, to see his wife attending to her ordinary household and social duties, although never fully restored to health. She tried to be cheerful and did not like to be thought an invalid. Often she would express an opinion on public affairs so sound and sensible as to bring forth the reply, 'Ida, I think you are right.' She manifested a wife's interest in all her husband's achievements and was wide awake to the issues of the day. Nevertheless, there was never a moment in McKinley's subsequent career when his mind was free from anxiety on her account, nor when she was not the object of his tenderest solicitude."

Katherine McKinley

Even in the midst of her own suffering, Ida insisted that he continue his legal and political career, and in 1876, McKinley became involved in a legal case that would turn out to have a profound impact on his political career. Olcott explained, "In March, 1876, a strike of coal-miners was declared in the Tuscarawas Valley. The operators undertook to break the strike by collecting miners in Cleveland and vicinity and transporting them to a mine in Stark County, a few miles south of Massillon. The property was managed by Rhodes & Company, of Cleveland, of which firm Marcus A. Hanna was the leading member. It was operated by George H. Warmington, a partner of Mr. Hanna. In April a second gang of strike-breakers was sent to the mine, and arrived just while the strikers were holding a meeting. The cry of 'scab' was instantly raised, and with a rush the strikers attacked the car, precipitating a general mêlée in which Mr. Warmington was assaulted and nearly killed. The whole district was thrown into a turmoil and the sheriff was obliged to call upon Governor Hayes for assistance. A company of militia was sent to the scene and succeeded in quelling the disorder, but not until after the strikers had set fire to the mines belonging to Hanna's firm. Many miners were arrested and taken to Canton for trial. With the public mind inflamed against the rioters, it was not easy for them to secure counsel. At length an appeal was made to McKinley. Upon investigation he found that many of the miners had been unjustly accused. He undertook their defense and pleaded so successfully that nearly all of them were acquitted. Realizing that the strike had made them nearly destitute, he refused to accept payment for his services. The operators were represented by Lynch and Day, the senior partner being McKinley's former opponent as a candidate for prosecuting attorney and the junior partner his lifelong friend and future cabinet officer, William R. Day." Most importantly, McKinley came to the attention of Mark Hanna, who was impressed with the young man despite being on the opposing side.

Hanna

McKinley in the 1870s

In 1876, McKinley campaigned for the Republican nomination for Ohio's 17th Congressional District, which he received in August 1876. He campaigned against the Democratic nominee mostly on his support for the protective tariff, and he ultimately won the election.

During his first term in Congress, McKinley became known for his strong and consistent defense of the protective tariff. The tariff primarily allowed American industries to develop by giving them a price advantage over foreign competitors in the domestic market, and McKinley constantly supported bills that raised tariffs and opposed those that lowered them. Olcott observed, "From the time of his first speech in Congress until the end of his life, McKinley sought to elaborate, clarify, and systematize the true 'American' policy of Protection. He laid down the principle, as its basis, that 'self-preservation is the first law of nature, as it is and should be of nations.' He insisted upon the paramount importance of the 'general welfare,' and that the country must be made independent in a 'broad and comprehensive sense,' strong, self-supporting, and self-sustaining. This was the teaching of Hamilton and Washington. He further laid down the cardinal principle of the Protectionist school in the words: 'It is our duty and we ought to protect as sacredly and assuredly the labor and industry of the United States as we would protect her honor from taint or her territory from invasion.'"

Soon after taking office on December 10, 1877. McKinley presented memorials from steel and iron companies in Canton, Massillon, Struthers, and Youngstown. The memorials requested "that Congress will take no action concerning a revision of tariff duties until after it shall have ascertained, by an official inquiry, the condition of the industries of the country, and the nature of such tariff legislation as in the opinion of practical business men would best promote the restoration of general prosperity."

One of his first speeches in Congress was in opposition to the Wood Tariff Bill, introduced by Democrat Congressman Fernando Wood of New York. McKinley opposed the bill because it proposed lowering tariff rates, reducing the protective nature of the tariff. McKinley said of the bill, "This bill not only impairs the revenues of the Government, but it is a blow well directed at the mining, the manufacturing, and the industrial classes of this country. It will not be denied that any material readjustment of the tariff system at this time is a delicate and hazardous undertaking, and should be approached, if at all, with great care and circumspection, with a thorough knowledge of the business and commerce of the country, their needs and relations, which it proposes to affect. Its consideration should be unencumbered by individual or sectional interests, and should be free from any attempt or desire to promote the interests of one class at the expense of the many. The highest good to the greatest number should guide any legislation which may be had. I believe if this rule should be adopted the proposed measure would find little favor in this House. I do not doubt that free trade, or its 'next of kin,' tariff reform, might be of temporary advantage to a very limited class of our population, and would be hailed with delight by the home importer and foreign manufacturer; but no one, I predict, who has thoughtfully considered the subject and its effects upon our present state and condition can fail to discern that free trade or tariff reform, introduced into this country now, would produce still further business depression and increased commercial paralyzation. Our once prosperous manufactories are barely able now, with the present duties upon imports, to keep their wheels in motion; and what, I ask, must become of them if the foreign-manufactured product which competes with the manufactured product of the United States shall be suffered to come into this country free of duty or at reduced rates of duty? Mr. Chairman, there can be but one result, which I shall endeavor to present later in the course of my remarks." The bill was defeated on June 5, 1878.

In 1882, McKinley spoke in the House concerning the appointment of a Tariff Commission: "The tariff question has again forced itself into prominence. While it has never ceased to be a question upon which the political parties of the country have made some declaration, yet for many years other issues have in a great measure determined party divisions and controlled party discipline. The last Presidential campaign brought recognition and discussion of this issue, and it may be fairly said that Republican advocacy of the protective principle contributed in no small degree to the success of the Republican National ticket. It can safely be asserted that the doctrine of a tariff for revenue and protection as against a tariff for revenue only is the dominant sentiment in the United States to-day; and if a vote upon that issue, with every other question eliminated, could be had, the majority would not only be large, but surprisingly large, for the protective principle."

In time, McKinley soon rose to prominence in Republican circles. When James Garfield was elected president in 1880, a vacancy opened on the Ways and Means Committee, and the question of who should fill Garfield's position was left to Garfield himself. Olcott described what happened next: "Samuel J. Randall, the Speaker, frankly said to them that he should be governed by the advice of General Gar field. Randall and Garfield, though leaders of opposing political parties, had served together for many years in the House, had been members of the same committees, were warm personal friends, and held each other in the highest esteem. Garfield named McKinley for the vacancy and Randall appointed him. There was some criticism that a man who had been in Congress only three years should receive an appointment so important, but there was no question of his ability. The thoroughness with which he had handled the subject of the Tariff in the debate on the Wood Bill had been convincing proof of that. Randall and Garfield both saw the desirability of placing such a man on the committee, where his unusual knowledge of the Tariff and his decided interest in the protective principle would be of the greatest service. The result showed that Garfield advised well and Randall acted wisely."

Randall

Garfield

The Election of 1880 was won by Garfield, and Republicans were a slender majority in the House, so McKinley kept a seat on the Ways and Means Committee. The Tariff Commission mentioned above was enacted by Congress in 1882, and the following year, the Commission recommended the reduction of tariff rates. Both the House and the Senate crafted their own bills incorporating the recommendations, which were reconciled in a conference committee.

When the bill was debated in the House, McKinley led the opposition to it. Olcott recorded one encounter with a free-trade representative, Congressman Springer: "McKinley was speaking of the hardships that result to labor from free trade, saying, 'I speak for the workingmen of my district, the workingmen of Ohio, and of the country,' when Springer interrupted with the uncalled-for remark, 'They did not speak for you very largely at the last election.' Quickly turning on his opponent, McKinley, with a flashing eye, but with no show of anger, replied impressively: 'Ah, my friend, my fidelity to my constituents is not measured by the support they give me! (Great applause..] I have convictions upon this subject which I would not surrender or refrain from advocating if ten thousand majority had been entered against me last October [renewed applause]; and if that is the standard of political morality and conviction and fidelity to duty which is practiced by the gentleman from Illinois, I trust that the next House will not do what I know they will not do, make him Speaker of the House.'"

When the 48th Congress was elected with the Democrats in the majority again, the Democrats introduced a new tariff bill calling for an across-the-board reduction in tariff rates, and McKinley once again led the charge against this legislation, known as the Morrison Tariff Bill. In a speech on April 30, 1884, McKinley said, "The bill reported from the Committee on Ways and Means is a proposition to reduce the duties upon all articles of imported merchandise, except those embraced in two schedules, to wit, spirits and silks, twenty per cent. It is to be a horizontal reduction, not a well matured and carefully considered revision. Its author makes no such claim for it, but confesses in his recent speech, that while a revision and adjustment are 'essential,' 'they are believed to be unattainable at the present session of Congress.' It admits of no exception or discrimination, except only that the proposed reduction shall not operate to reduce the duty below the rate at which any article was dutiable under the tariff act of 1861, commonly called 'the Morrill tariff,' and in no case shall cotton goods pay a higher rate of duty than forty per cent ad valorem, and wools and woolens a higher rate than sixty per cent ad valorem, and metals a higher rate of duty than fifty per cent ad valorem. With these exceptions and qualifications only eighty percent of the duties now imposed by law are to be collected under the bill we are now considering. The friends of this measure have felt called upon in advance to apologize for the smallness of the proposed reduction, and attempt to conciliate that large majority of their party which is in favor of the English system by declaring that this is only a step, and the first step, in the direction of the ultimate enactment of a pure revenue tariff. It is the first move toward the destruction of that system of tariff duties which has been recognized in this Government from its foundation as essential to its revenues and the proper care of its own industries. It is not because they are favorable to protection, even incidentally, that only twenty per cent reduction is proposed, but because, believing this is all they can accomplish this year, they invite all the friends of tariff reform to join them, with the assurance that next year, and for the following years, additional steps will be taken which will ultimately bring our tariff taxation to a strictly revenue basis; which means a tax upon tea and coffee and such other articles as we can not produce or manufacture in the United States, and the release of all others from customs duties."

By 1886 McKinley, was widely viewed as one of the leaders of the Republican Party in Ohio. Along with Senator John Sherman and Governor Joseph B. Foraker, McKinley shaped the party in the state, and his strong relationship with those two attracted the attention of Mark Hanna. At the 1888 Republican National Convention, however, Foraker earned the ire of McKinley, Sherman, and Hanna when he abandoned Sherman's attempt to gain the nomination for president in favor of Senator James G. Blaine of Maine. The nomination eventually went to Benjamin Harrison, but in the bitterness that followed, the Ohio Republican Party split between a faction aligned with McKinley, Sherman and Hanna, and one aligned with Foraker. The major effect on

McKinley's political future was the support that Hanna gave him after 1888.

Foraker

McKinley's Fall and Rise

When the Republicans returned to the majority in 1889, McKinley ran for Speaker of the House, only to lose to Thomas B. Reed of Maine. In the wake of that, Reed gave McKinley the chair of the Ways and Means Committee, and it was in that position that McKinley pushed through the House his signature piece of legislation, the McKinley Tariff of 1890. The legislation enshrined McKinley's protectionist beliefs, raising the average duty on imports to 50% while eliminating duties on sugar, molasses, tea, coffee, and hides. In support of his own bill, McKinley asserted, "But, Mr. Chairman, in the presence of our magnificent domestic commerce, the commerce along our inland seas, our lakes and rivers and great railroad lines, why need we vex ourselves about foreign commerce? The domestic trade of the United States is 95% of the whole of our trade. Nowhere is the progress of the country so manifest as in this wonderful growth and development. The water carriage of the United States along its coasts and its rivers is five times greater than the foreign commerce of the United States. Why, the movement of tonnage through the Detroit River in 1889 was 10,000,000 tons more than the total registered entries and clearances at all the seaports of the United States, and it was 3,000,000 tons in excess of the combined foreign and coastwise registered tonnage of the ports of Liverpool and London. What higher testimony do we want of the growth of our internal commerce?...If the United States would give the same encouragement to her merchant marine and her steamship lines as is given by other nations to their ships this commerce on the seas under the American flag would increase and multiply. When the United States will expend from her treasury from five to six millions a year for that purpose, as do France and Great Britain to maintain their steamship lines, our ships will plough every sea in successful competition with the ships of the world...With me this position is a deep conviction, not a theory, I believe in it and thus warmly advocate it because enveloped in it are my country's highest development and greatest prosperity; out of it come the greatest gains to the people, the greatest comforts to the masses, the widest encouragement for manly aspirations, with the largest rewards, dignifying and elevating our citizenship, upon which the safety and purity and permanence of our political system depend."

The McKinley Tariff passed the House 164-142, with all but two Republicans voting for the bill. In a modified form, the bill passed the Senate and went into effect on October 6, 1890.

The country's reaction to the McKinley Tariff was swift and negative. With elections only a month away, Democrats and their allies heaped derision on the measure. Olcott, clearly a supporter of McKinley, described the reaction: "Never before had a tariff bill created such an uproar throughout the country. Never was such a measure so persistently misrepresented. Never were the voters more hopelessly befuddled. Never was their judgment so violently warped by false predictions of dire calamity. Unscrupulous dealers marked up the prices of their goods, frequently increasing those upon which the McKinley Act had made no change or had even made reductions. It was all the same to them. The new Tariff has made everything higher, they said, though as a matter of fact it had been in force so short a time that its effects were not as yet appreciable. In McKinley's own district, a few days before the election, tin peddlers were hired to go into the rural districts. They offered coffee pots at $1.50, and tin cups, worth about five cents, for twenty-five cents or more. Everybody was horrified. Of course no sales were made, but the lesson was well impressed that the dreadful McKinley Act had greatly increased the cost of everything."

The election was a disaster for Republicans in general and McKinley in particular. Not only were Democrats swept into a majority in the House, McKinley lost his own seat. He wrote an editorial concerning his defeat in the Canton *Evening Repository* that was published November 8, 1890, and in it he complained, "The elections this year were determined upon a false issue. A conspiracy between importers, many of whom were not even citizens of the United States, and the free-traders of this country, to raise prices and charge it upon the McKinley Bill, was successful. But conspiracies are short-lived and soon expire. This one has already been laid bare, and the infamy of it will still further appear. Merchants are already advertising, now that the election is over, to sell at even lower prices than before the passage of the McKinley Bill. The trick has won this time. The conspiracy has triumphed. But the people who have been duped will not forget. Nor will the friends of protection lower their flag or raise the British flag. The result this year is but history repeating itself. Every great measure for the benefit of the people and the country, passed immediately before an election, has been temporarily disastrous to the party responsible for it."

In the aftermath of his defeat, McKinley answered the call of many Ohio Republicans and sought the party's nomination for governor. While the position did not have much power at the time, it was important in national politics due to Ohio's role as a swing state. He won the 1891 election by 20,000 votes, and in 1892, he was mentioned by many disaffected Republicans as a replacement for President Benjamin Harrison. Harrison's campaign managers arranged for McKinley to be the permanent convention chairman at the 1892 Republican National Convention, thus taking McKinley out of the mix. Nevertheless, Hanna set up an unofficial campaign headquarters for McKinley, though they made no active effort to recruit delegates. In the end, McKinley finished third in the balloting behind Harrison and Blaine. McKinley campaigned for Harrison in the fall, but the unpopular Harrison lost to Grover Cleveland, who became the only president to date to be elected to a second non-consecutive term.

The defeated Republicans considered McKinley as the most likely candidate in 1896, and in the intervening years, McKinley's stock in national Republican politics continued to increase. He won easy reelection in 1893 and campaigned for Republican candidates during the 1894 midterms, with many of the candidates he campaigned for winning their elections. He procured a Republican successor as governor in 1895 and was able to get his old foe Foraker elected to the Senate. McKinley's support was crucial for Foraker, because in return, Foraker promised to back McKinley's subsequent run for the presidency.

The Election of 1896 is considered by historians as one of the pivotal elections in American history. From the beginning, McKinley was seen as the most likely Republican candidate, though it's unclear when he began to eye a run for the office. Hanna was key to McKinley's campaign, both through his money and his organizational abilities. Hanna's early efforts put other Republican contenders, namely Speaker Thomas B. Reed and Iowa Senator William B. Allison, at a great disadvantage. Stanley Jones, in his study of the election, noted, "Another feature common to the Reed and Allison campaigns was their failure to make headway against the tide which was running toward McKinley. In fact, both campaigns from the moment they were launched were in retreat. The calm confidence with which each candidate claimed the support of his own section [of the country] soon gave way to... bitter accusations that Hanna by winning support for McKinley in their sections had violated the rules of the game."

McKinley: "Please, mister, may I have the core?"
Hanna: "Git away, boy; they ain't goin' to be no core."

By Homer C. Davenport, the New York "Journal."

A cartoon insinuating that Hanna would be the real president if McKinley was elected

An 1896 cartoon depicting McKinley and Hanna carving up the presidency like a Thanksgiving turkey

McKinley quickly rejected the offers from Republican bosses such as Senators Thomas Platt of New York and Matthew Quay of Pennsylvania to guarantee his nomination in exchange for promises of patronage positions for political loyalists. Hanna supported this, and the duo focused attention on the small Republican Party in the South and the border states, quickly gaining delegates from those states. Party bosses were still determined to deny McKinley a first ballot victory, but thanks to Hanna's efforts, particularly in Illinois and Indiana, by the time of the convention in St. Louis in June, McKinley had a majority of delegates already pledged to him. He won the nomination on the first ballot, with the delegation from Ohio putting him over the top.

McKinley was at home in Canton, following the voting by telephone. Olcott described the scene: "At 5 P.M. the operator at the head of the stairs announced that the roll-call had been ordered. A tense feeling of anxious but hopeful expectation filled the entire household. One by one the States were called, in alphabetical order, and their votes announced. To nominate on the first ballot would require 453% votes. By the time Ohio had been reached, the score-cards had already recorded 42.1% votes for McKinley, nearly the required number. Then the operator called out, "Ohio, forty-six for McKinley," and everybody present knew that the work had been completed by the solid vote of their own State. The Major arose, crossed the hall into the parlor, and gently kissed his wife and his mother. The neighbors crowded about to offer their congratulations. They had scarcely had time to do this before the street before the house was blocked with enthusiastic townsmen. A prominent citizen made an address of congratulation and Major McKinley, mounting a chair, delivered the first speech of the campaign. A few minutes later two thousand citizens of Alliance, twenty miles away, arrived before the house. They had started on a special train the moment the vote of Ohio decided the result, and reached the Governor's house in forty-five minutes. At 7.15 nineteen carloads of people arrived from Massillon, packed so closely that men were clinging to the sides and riding on the tops of the coaches. At 7.40 four trains of ten cars each brought four thousand people from Akron. These were followed by a special train from Carrollton, and at ten o'clock a delegation ar rived from Niles, the birthplace of McKinley, sixty miles away. Between five o'clock and midnight at least fifty thousand people listened to speeches by the candidate and many of them were personally greeted by him. Thus was inaugurated, spontaneously, on the very day of the convention, what proved to be one of the most remarkable episodes in the history of American politics, – the rush of hundreds of thousands of voters to hear a presidential candidate speak from his own doorstep. A movement that started out of the enthusiasm of his nearest neighbors was encouraged by McKinley and his astute manager, until it reached unprecedented proportions."

McKinley at home in 1896

McKinley during the campaign on his front porch in 1896

McKinley faced the Democratic nominee, the populist firebrand and orator William Jennings Bryan, who made free silver the cornerstone of his campaign, in contrast to the Republican's traditional stance on the gold standard. The two men could not be more different, and Bryan's campaign was in many ways the first modern presidential campaign, with the Democrat traveling the country by train, speaking to crowds personally rather than sending surrogates. Olcott commented, "Major McKinley, on the contrary, felt that the dignity of the presidential office was such as to preclude the candidate from rushing about over the country in a frenzied hunt for votes. There were many who urged him to meet Mr. Bryan's activity by a counter-move, but he persistently refused. His action was justified even from the politician's viewpoint, for he had discovered a better method. He remained at home and the people came to him. Delegations from all parts of the country marched daily through the streets of Canton to the candidate's home on Market Street. From morning to night he addressed them from the front porch. His speeches, though often introduced with pleasantries, were solid arguments founded on fact and addressed to the sober judgment of the people. Though speaking, physically, to a crowd that overflowed the lawn and street in front of his house, he knew that he was in reality addressing millions of his fellow citizens, for his speeches were printed in full in the newspapers throughout the country. Every word was carefully prepared. No utterance required an apology. There was no lack of variety of interest, as day by day he appealed to the conscience of his countrymen and reached their intelligence by a fair, calm, and persuasive presentation of the truth as he saw it. Every speech strengthened his cause and increased the popular respect for him."

Bryan appealed to rural voters in the South and West who saw free silver as a way of raising the prices they received for their products on the market. McKinley appealed to urban voters and industrial workers by emphasizing the role the gold standard played in stabilizing prices for consumers and the role the protective tariff played in supporting American jobs. In November, McKinley romped to a clear Electoral College majority over Bryan, which, in the view of many historians, broke the deadlock between the Republicans and Democrats and ushered in a Republican dominance in national politics that only ended with Franklin D. Roosevelt winning in 1932.

McKinley's Presidency

McKinley was sworn in to on March 4, 1897, and Olcott listed some of the challenges he faced upon coming into office: "The country was suffering from a widespread industrial depression. The Tariff of 1894 had not only greatly unsettled the manufacturing and commercial interests, but had failed to provide sufficient revenue for the expenses of the Government. A steadily increasing fear had spread over the country, lest the gold standard should not be maintained...Nor were the domestic problems the only ones requiring serious thought. The Cuban question was rapidly reaching a point when action of some kind on the part of the United States would soon be inevitable, and in addition there was the annexation of Hawaii still awaiting settlement, besides a pending treaty of arbitration with Great Britain, and numerous other matters of minor importance."

During his inauguration, McKinley addressed the various problems facing the country, telling the crowd, "The responsibilities of the high trust to which I have been called--always of grave importance--are augmented by the prevailing business conditions entailing idleness upon willing labor and loss to useful enterprises. The country is suffering from industrial disturbances from which speedy relief must be had. Our financial system needs some revision; our money is all good now, but its value must not further be threatened. It should all be put upon an enduring basis, not subject to easy attack, nor its stability to doubt or dispute. Our currency should continue under the supervision of the Government. The several forms of our paper money offer, in my judgment, a constant embarrassment to the Government and a safe balance in the Treasury. Therefore I believe it necessary to devise a system which, without diminishing the circulating medium or offering a premium for its contraction, will present a remedy for those arrangements which, temporary in their nature, might well in the years of our prosperity have been displaced by wiser provisions. With adequate revenue secured, but not until then, we can enter upon such changes in our fiscal laws as will, while insuring safety and volume to our money, no longer impose upon the Government the necessity of maintaining so large a gold reserve, with its attendant and inevitable temptations to speculation. Most of our financial laws are the outgrowth of experience and trial, and should not be amended without investigation and demonstration of the wisdom of the proposed changes. We must be both 'sure we are right' and 'make haste slowly.' If, therefore, Congress, in its wisdom, shall deem it expedient to create a commission to take under early consideration the revision of our coinage, banking and currency laws, and give them that exhaustive, careful and dispassionate examination that their importance demands, I shall cordially concur in such action. If such power is vested in the president, it is my purpose to appoint a commission of prominent, well-informed citizens of different parties, who will command public confidence, both on account of their ability and special fitness for the work. Business experience and public training may thus be combined, and the patriotic zeal of the friends of the country be so directed that such a report will be made as to receive the support of all parties, and our finances cease to be the subject of mere partisan contention. The experiment is, at all events, worth a trial, and, in my opinion, it can but prove beneficial to the entire country."

McKinley concluded his speech with the following: "In conclusion, I congratulate the country upon the fraternal spirit of the people and the manifestations of good will everywhere so apparent. The recent election not only most fortunately demonstrated the obliteration of sectional or geographical lines, but to some extent also the prejudices which for years have distracted our councils and marred our true greatness as a nation. The triumph of the people, whose verdict is carried into effect today, is not the triumph of one section, nor wholly of one party, but of all sections and all the people. The North and the South no longer divide on the old lines, but upon principles and policies; and in this fact surely every lover of the country can find cause for true felicitation. Let us rejoice in and cultivate this spirit; it is ennobling and will be both a gain and a blessing to our beloved country. It will be my constant aim to do nothing, and permit nothing to be done, that will arrest or disturb this growing sentiment of unity and cooperation, this revival of esteem and affiliation which now animates so many thousands in both the old antagonistic sections, but I shall cheerfully do everything possible to promote and increase it. Let me again repeat the words of the oath administered by the Chief Justice which, in their respective spheres, so far as applicable, I would have all my countrymen observe: 'I will faithfully execute the office of President of the United States, and will, to the best of my ability, preserve, protect, and defend the Constitution of the United States.' This is the obligation I have reverently taken before the Lord Most High. To keep it will be my single purpose, my constant prayer; and I shall confidently rely upon the forbearance and assistance of all the people in the discharge of my solemn responsibilities."

For all of McKinley's focus during his political career on issues of trade and monetary policy, his first term as president is most notable for events overseas. It was during this period that many in the United States believed the time had come for the nation to join Britain, France, Germany, and others as an imperial power. This group believed that America had outgrown the traditions of leaders like Washington and Madison who looked at the country's involvement overseas with skepticism. A modern industrial country needed a modern military and needed overseas possessions.

Olcott noted, "The administration of President McKinley will stand in history as one of the great transition periods in the progress of the country. As Washington successfully inaugurated the self-government of the American people and Lincoln was able to preserve it in the hour of greatest danger, so McKinley, with a patience and wisdom akin to Lincoln's, and with a breadth of vision impossible in the time of Washington, successfully guided the affairs of state during that difficult period when the United States was being transformed from the position of an isolated nation to one of vastly greater influence among the powers of the world. It was the hand of Destiny that conferred upon him this unique distinction...He will be known in history...as the president who successfully conducted a war with Spain, after doing all in his power to avert it, and then, accepting the larger duties to humanity which the victorious result had thrust upon the Nation, entered with firm step and courageous heart upon the new era of expansion and international responsibility."

The question of the annexation of Hawaii was the first issue that confronted McKinley concerning the expansion of the United States overseas. The potential annexation had occupied the country since 1893, when American merchants on the island deposed the last Queen of Hawaii and established the Republic of Hawaii. Representatives of the Republic had requested annexation, and President Harrison had submitted an annexation treaty to the Senate for approval, but it had been withdrawn by Cleveland. McKinley, on June 16, 1897, submitted a new treaty to the Senate and included a report from Secretary of State John Sherman, part of which read, "Hawaii sends to the United States not a commission representing a successful revolution, but the accredited plenipotentiary of a constituted and firmly established sovereign state."

Some in the Senate objected, saying the United States had no legal or moral right to annex the territory of an independent state and that there would be no strategic advantage to the United States to have Hawaii as a possession. The treaty was defeated, but during the Spanish-American War, part of which included fighting in the Philippines, the strategic value of Hawaii became clearer. A joint Congressional resolution providing for the annexation of the islands passed the House on June 15, 1898 and the Senate on July 6, 1898, with McKinley signing it the next day. On April 30, 1900, Hawaii became a Territory of the United States.

Meanwhile, Cuba had concerned McKinley since his first day in office. F. E. Chadwick wrote of the island, "The late war was but the culmination of difficulties which had their seed in the Peace of 1763. They sprang into life twenty years later with the advent on the world's stage of the American Union; remained in full vigor for half a century thereafter with scarcely an interval of repose, and waxed and waned for seventy-five years more, until finally war came in 1898 to remove the last cause of friction. Few of the one hundred and fifteen years from 1783 to 1898 were free from bitterness of feeling. The war was thus but a final episode in a century of diplomatic ill-feeling, sometimes dormant, but more often dangerously acute."

The intermittent campaign waged by Cuban rebels against Spanish colonial rule erupted in 1895 into a full-fledged war for Cuban independence. American public opinion favored the rebels, especially as Spain took harsher and harsher measures against the rebels, and there were increasing calls for war against Spain to liberate Cuba. McKinley sympathized with the rebels, but he favored peaceful negotiations to convince Spain to grant Cuba independence or autonomy. Negotiations between the United States and Cuba in 1897, however, soon revealed that Spain would never grant Cuba independence, and the Cuban rebels would not accept anything less. Agitation for war increased, stirred by the exaggerated reports published in the newspapers owned by William Randolph Hearst.

As the conditions in Cuba worsened into 1898, McKinley was criticized for appearing reluctant to act. McKinley, in a conversation with Senator Fairbanks, expressed his concerns about war, something he had firsthand knowledge of: "It isn't the money that will be spent nor the property that will be destroyed, if war comes, that concerns me; but the thought of human suffering that must come into thousands of homes throughout the country is almost overwhelming."

On the evening of February 15, 1898, at around 9:40 p.m., the twinkling, tranquil water of Havana's harbor had been rocked by a thunderous explosion. An American battleship, the USS *Maine*, captained by Charles D. Sigsbee, burst into flames, with the bottom of the vessel completely disintegrating due to a blast so powerful that it shook the earth and shattered almost all the windows of neighboring buildings. 250 enlisted soldiers and two officers perished in the explosion, and another 14 succumbed to their fatal injuries days later.

The USS _Maine_ entering Havana Harbor three weeks before the explosion

A picture of the wreckage

Over 115 years later, the explosion of the *Maine* is perhaps best remembered for being associated with yellow journalism and as the primary cause of the Spanish-American War, which makes it somewhat fitting that the explosion itself remains an unsolved mystery. In spite of the increasing calls for intervention in Cuba, McKinley calmly insisted that a court of inquiry determine if the explosion was the result of an accident, or if it was a deliberate act. He told Senator Fairbanks, "I don't propose to be swept off my feet by the catastrophe. My duty is plain. We must learn the truth and endeavor, if possible, to fix the responsibility. The country can afford to withhold its judgment and not strike an avenging blow until the truth is known. The Administration will go on preparing for war, but still hoping to avert it. It will not be plunged into war until it is ready for it. Responsibility for the catastrophe in Havana Harbor will be searched thoroughly and with all reasonable dispatch, and when the responsibility is fixed, the Government will be prepared to act, and if the facts warrant it will act with resolution — but not before."

There was never another official public investigation carried out by the American government after 1911, but several private investigations have sought to answer the enduring mystery, and the most recent efforts have theorized that the explosion was an accident caused by burning coal.

A 1974 investigation led by Admiral Hyman G. Rickover was the first major study to suggest that a spontaneous combustion of coal in one of the ship's bunkers triggered the explosion of an adjacent magazine, which then caused the heavy majority of the damage.

On March 20, the investigation concluded that the *Maine* was the victim of an underwater mine. McKinley continued to try negotiations with Spain for Cuban independence, but Spain refused all proposals. On April 11, McKinley transmitted a message to Congress. After summarizing the situation in Cuba and his efforts at negotiating a peaceful solution, he said the following: "The only hope of relief and repose from a condition which can no longer be endured is the enforced pacification of Cuba. In the name of humanity, in the name of civilization, in behalf of endangered American interests which gives us the right and the duty to speak and to act, the war in Cuba must stop. In view of these facts and of these considerations, I ask the Congress to authorize and empower the president to take measure to secure a full and final termination of hostilities between the Government of Spain and the people of Cuba, and to secure in the island the establishment of a stable government, capable of maintaining order and observing its international obligations, insuring peace and tranquility and the security of its citizens as well as our own, and to use the military and naval forces of the United States as may be necessary for these purposes. And in the interest of humanity and to aid in preserving the lives of the starving people of the island I recommend that the distribution of food and supplies be continued, and that an appropriation be made out of the public Treasury to supplement the charity of our citizens. The issue is now with the Congress. It is a solemn responsibility. I have exhausted every effort to relieve the intolerable condition of affairs which is at our doors. Prepared to execute every obligation imposed upon me by the Constitution and the law, I await your action."

Although there were conflicting conclusions and the Sampson Board was unable to give a definitive answer about who was responsible for the explosion, Americans who constantly read the lurid tales published daily in national and local newspapers largely blamed the Spanish government in Cuba and insisted that the United States go to war to help the Cuban rebels oust their Spanish rulers once and for all. The House and the Senate passed a declaration of war on Spain on April 20, 1898, and McKinley signed the declaration the same day. The declaration included an amendment proposed by Senator Henry M. Teller of Colorado designed to garner the support of anti-imperialists which promised that the United States would not annex Cuba and would withdraw military forces once Cuba's independence was obtained.

A large military force consisting of Regular Army units and volunteer companies gathered at Tampa, Florida, awaiting embarkation to Cuba. Although it encountered difficulties, the force finally sailed from Tampa on June 20, landing near Santiago de Cuba on June 22. After a small skirmish at Las Guasimas on June 24, U.S. forces battled the Spanish at the Battle of San Juan Hill on July 2. The battle resulted in heavy casualties on both sides, with the Americans emerging victorious.

The defeat of the Spanish forces on land was followed the next day by the destruction of the ships of the Spanish Caribbean squadron by the U.S. Navy's North Atlantic Squadron. The city of Santiago surrendered to U.S. forces on July 17, placing Cuba in American control. An invasion of the Spanish colony of the island of Puerto Rico met little resistance.

While victorious in Cuba, American operations against Spanish possessions in the Pacific were even more successful. Commodore George Dewey's Asiatic Squadron destroyed the Spanish fleet at the Battle of Manila Bay in the Philippines, and with that, the fight against Spain went from being a war to liberate Cuba for the Cuban people to being a war to expand American possessions overseas. By the time U.S. troops landed in the Philippines in June 1898, McKinley had decided that Spain would surrender the islands to the United States as a prize of war.

Though the war with Spain was a very short conflict with relatively few American casualties (more soldiers died because of tropical disease than fell in battle), McKinley still felt the strain of all the losses. George B. Cortelyou, McKinley's personal secretary, recorded in his diary, "Sunday, May 15, 1898. The President is again looking careworn, the color having faded from his cheeks and the rings being once more noticeable about his eyes. The strain upon him is terrible. Un certainty as to the whereabouts of the Cape Verde fleet; the growing unrest and threatening character of the European situation, — these, coupled with the many difficulties constantly arising as a result of the short - sighted policy which for so long a time has been pursued by Congress, leaving the country poorly prepared for hostilities, make the burden upon the Executive shoulders a heavy one. Added to these things is the struggle for place among the ambitious gentlemen who desire to serve their country in high - salaried and high - titled positions. And then, too, the present conditions are attended by the usual differences and bickerings among the officers of the army and navy, which in certain high quarters are altogether too apparent."

On August 12 Spain agreed to a ceasefire, and peace treaty negotiations began in Paris on October 1, 1898. McKinley had sent instructions to the U.S. negotiators which said in part, "It is my wish that throughout the negotiations entrusted to the Commission the purpose and spirit with which the United States accepted the unwelcome necessity of war should be kept constantly in view. We took up arms only in obedience to the dictates of humanity and in the fulfillment of high public and moral obligations. We had no design of aggrandizement and no ambition of conquest. Through the long course of repeated representations which preceded and aimed to avert the struggle, and in the final arbitrament of force, this country was impelled solely by the purpose of relieving grievous wrongs and removing long - existing conditions which disturbed its tranquillity, which shocked the moral sense of mankind, and which could no longer be endured. It is my earnest wish that the United States in making peace should follow the same high rule of conduct which guided it in facing war. It should be as scrupulous and magnanimous in the concluding settlement as it was just and humane in its original action. The luster and the moral strength attaching to a cause which can be confidently rested upon the considerate judgment of the world should not under any illusion of the hour be dimmed by ulterior designs which might tempt us into excessive demands or into an adventurous departure on untried paths. It is believed that the true glory and the enduring interests of the country will most surely be served if an unselfish duty conscientiously accepted and a signal triumph honorably achieved shall be crowned by such an example of moderation, restraint, and reason in victory as best comports with the traditions and character of our enlightened Republic."

The negotiations culminated on December 18, and as a result of the treaty, the United States acquired Puerto Rico, the Philippines, and Guam. Spain relinquished its claims to Cuba, and in return, the United States paid Spain $20 million.

Despite the lopsided nature of the war and the terms of the treaty, McKinley had difficulty getting the treaty approved by the Senate. Treaties require a two-thirds majority for approval, a number the president had difficulty reaching because about a third of the Senate opposed the provisions acquiring the former Spanish possessions in the Pacific and Puerto Rico. Senator Henry Cabot Lodge, who would later lead opposition to another treaty from another president, asserted, "Take now the other alternative. Suppose we reject the treaty or strike out the clause relating to the Philippines. That will hand the islands back to Spain; and I cannot conceive that any American should be willing to do that. Suppose we reject the treaty; what follows? Let us look at it practically. We continue the state of war and every sensible man in the country, every business interest, desires the reestablishment of peace in law as well as in fact. At the same time we repudiate the president and his action before the whole world, and the repudiation of the president in such a matter as this is, to my mind, the humiliation of the United States in the eyes of civilized mankind and brands us a people in capable of great affairs or of taking rank where we belong, as one of the greatest of the great world powers…The President cannot be sent back across the Atlantic in the person of his commissioners, hat in hand, to say to Spain, with bated breath, ' I am here in obedience to the mandate of a minority of one third of the Senate to tell you that we have been too victorious, and that you have yielded us too much, and that I am very sorry that I took the Philippines from you. I do not think that any American President would do that, or that any American would wish him to."

The Senate eventually ratified the Treaty 57-27, one vote above two-thirds. Ironically, it was William Jennings Bryan, who preferred any treaty to war, who was able to persuade enough Democrats to support the bill and allow it to pass.

Thanks to the victories in the war against Spain and the general prosperity the country was experiencing because of his economic policies, McKinley was considered a sure bet for reelection in 1900. The Democrats nominated Bryan again, with the Republicans nominating McKinley on the first ballot.

Thus, the only real contest among Republicans came about because Vice President Garret Hobart died in 1899. McKinley left the choice of choosing Hobart's successor to the party, and party insiders made a fateful choice.

In 1897, shortly after McKinley had taken office, he recognized Theodore Roosevelt's strengths and appointed him Assistant Secretary of the Navy after Senator Henry Cabot Lodge of Massachusetts reportedly suggested Roosevelt for the job. In many respects, the former New York Police Commissioner seemed an odd choice for the Navy, and Roosevelt had no experience whatsoever with ship building. However, back in his college days, he had written *The Naval War of 1812*, a heavily researched and authoritative account of the naval warfare during that war. Roosevelt dissected all aspects of naval warfare, from the size of ships and guns to the command structures of the warring sides' navies, and it is still considered one of the most comprehensive histories of the War of 1812 today. The book undoubtedly helped assure McKinley that Roosevelt was suited to the task.

When Roosevelt assumed his position as Assistant Secretary, he encountered a Navy that was poorly built and unprepared for warfare. This was especially concerning because Roosevelt (rightly) believed war with Spain was imminent. It was as Assistant Secretary of the Navy that Roosevelt first envisioned the U.S. strengthening its sphere of influence in the Western Hemisphere, and the creation of the Panama Canal first came to his mind during this time. To his dismay, however, Roosevelt encountered many in the government who thought preparing for a war would bring on the war itself.

Upon his return from Cuba after the Spanish-American War, Roosevelt was quickly recognized as an ideal option to be New York's governor. The Republicans in New York had been heavily divided by pro-machine and anti-machine elements, and the party had fallen on hard times throughout much of the state. To win in 1898, it needed a strong and popular candidate, and Roosevelt was the perfect solution.

In the general election campaign, Roosevelt took on the Tammany Hall boss who was backing his Democratic opponent. This proved a narrowly effective strategy, and Roosevelt won the election with a narrow margin of victory. He won a plurality of 49% to his Democratic opponent's nearly 48%.

Roosevelt's time as governor was busy, and it was defined by some of the same conflicts he encountered as Police Commissioner and on the Civil Service Commission. Once again, Roosevelt concentrated on rooting out crime and greed while improving the lot of working Americans. To achieve these goals, Governor Roosevelt's legislative agenda took on the state's political machines and large corporations directly. A former civil servant himself, Roosevelt ensured that New York's Civil Service Law was reenacted after being terminated by the prior governor.

Roosevelt's New York enemies hoped to rid the state of their progressive governor, but that would be easier said than done. After all, Governor Roosevelt was very popular and would undoubtedly be tough to beat as an incumbent in 1902. With that in mind, machine and corporate interests devised an interesting solution in the summer of 1900 - at the Republican National Convention in Philadelphia, the New York machine leaders decided to promote Roosevelt as a candidate for the vice presidency, because doing so would remove him from New York. In a way, it made sense since Vice President Roosevelt would have an insignificant influence over state and national politics. In other words, Roosevelt's enemies in New York figured that making him McKinley's underling would turn him into a nobody.

Initially, the machinists, led by Senator Thomas Platt of New York, encountered a problem: McKinley's campaign chief, Mark Hanna, did not think Roosevelt would make a good addition to the Republican ticket. The machinists, however, managed to convince Hanna and most other delegations at the convention that Roosevelt was the perfect addition to the ticket. For his part, Roosevelt was initially unsure of the position, and while many thought it would end his political career, Roosevelt wasn't even sure that was a bad thing.

After some convincing, Roosevelt accepted the nomination, and on November 6, 1900, McKinley and Roosevelt won the election with the largest victory for any Republican since 1872.

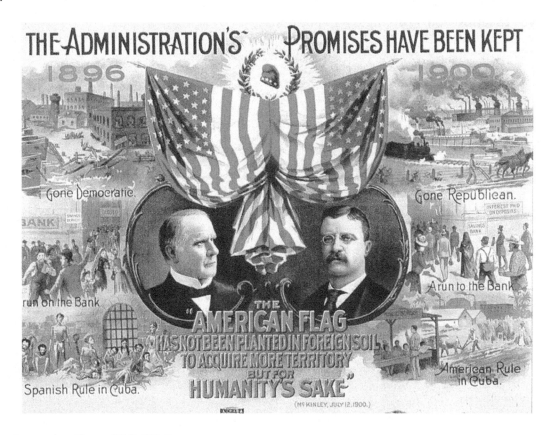

The Assassination of McKinley

Friday, September 6, 1901, dawned bright and clear for McKinley, both literally and figuratively. Just months after he had been reelected, he was looking forward to the enjoyable duty of once again visiting the Pan American Exposition, a symbol of all he believed the country was and could be.

That morning's timetable called for him to visit the Temple of Music. According to one exposition guide, "The Temple of Music is the center for musical interests at the Exposition. Its architecture is a free treatment of the Spanish Renaissance, it being octagonal in form, with pavilions at the corners. The grand entrance is at the corner of the Esplanade and Court of Fountains, the spacious courts upon which most of the principal buildings of the Exposition have their frontage. The cornice and balustrade are of elaborate composition, the latter bearing names familiar to the musical world. The interior of the temple is particularly fine in its sculptural and color decorations. The exterior of the building is ornate in architectural features and groups of sculpture designed to illustrate the purpose and character of the building. The great organ in the Temple of Music was built by Emmons Howard of Westfield, Mass., and cost $15,000. Concerts are held in the Temple every afternoon and evening. They are of a varied nature, but the high standard is maintained throughout. There are three band stands on the Exposition grounds, one in the rear, or north of the Electric Tower, in the center of the Sunken Gardens, and two in the Grand Esplanade, which will hold 250,000 people. Upwards of twenty bands have been employed to furnish music during the Exposition."

A postcard depicting the Temple of Music

A picture of the Temple of Music taken at the expo

   McKinley had other reasons to be optimistic about the day, as he was still riding the tidal wave of applause he had received the previous day for what many considered to be his greatest speech. In it, he had praised the exposition and all like it, saying, "The quest for trade is an incentive to men of business to devise, invent, improve and economize in the cost of production. Business life, whether among ourselves or with other people, is ever a sharp struggle for success. It will be none the less so in the future. Without competition we would be clinging to the clumsy and antiquated processes of farming and manufacture and the methods of business of long ago, and the twentieth would be no further advanced than the eighteenth century. But though commercial competitors we are, commercial enemies we must not be. The Pan-American Exposition has done its work thoroughly, presenting in its exhibits evidences of the highest skill and illustrating the progress of the human family in the western hemisphere. This portion of the earth has no cause for humiliation for the part it has performed in the march of civilization. It has not accomplished everything; far from it. It has simply done its best, and without vanity or boastfulness and recognizing the manifold achievements of others, it invites the friendly rivalry of all the powers in the peaceful pursuits of trade and commerce, and will co-operate with all in advancing the highest and best interests of humanity."

A picture of McKinley taken on September 5, 1901

Trade was important to McKinley, who had built his presidency on pulling the United States out of its first major economic depression. The Panic of 1893, occurring just a few years before he came into office, had caused serious problems for the nation, which was still recovering from the depths of the Civil War. Indeed, one of the men in Buffalo that day, anarchist Leon Czolgosz, had lost his job during the Panic of 1893, which drove him towards embracing anarchy in the first place. Thanks in large measure to McKinley's guidance, however, the country was once again on solid economic ground and experiencing the type of boom that typically only comes along once or twice in a generation.

Czolgosz

Presidential security in 1901 was quite lax by modern standards. For instance, while in Buffalo, the president and his wife stayed at the house of John Milburn, the president of the exposition. McKinley enjoyed the informality of someone's home and, always solicitous of his wife, felt that Ida was more comfortable away from prying eyes, but while the Secret Service had no problem securing the home, some felt that having the president walk around the fairgrounds with the rest of the crowds was not a good idea. George Cortelyou, McKinley's personal secretary, was particularly concerned about the president's visit to the Temple of Music and repeatedly tried to have that stop removed from the program altogether, but McKinley insisted on putting it back in.

Defeated but not deterred, Cortelyou telegraphed the exposition staff and had them arrange extra security for McKinley's tour of the Temple.

Ida McKinley

Cortelyou

JOHN G. MILBURN
President of the Pan-American Exposition.

Milburn

The Milburn house

By the time he arrived at the Temple of Music, McKinley and his wife had enjoyed a tour of Niagara Falls and returned by train to Buffalo. Ida was not feeling well and decided not to accompany her husband to the public reception at the Temple, but McKinley arrived there at around 4:00 p.m., basking in the glow of applause as those in line waited to shake his hand.

Randolph Keim was there that day and had a good view of the events that subsequently transpired. The next day, he recorded his observations, beginning with a description of the president's arrival: "Hearing the cheers of the vast throng of people who were awaiting the arrival of the president at the exposition grounds, I sauntered across the esplanade to view the enthusiastic demonstrations which were being made as the procession passed along the western drive of the esplanade in a southerly direction from the railroad gate. The Presidential party arrived at the Music Temple about three minutes past 4 o'clock, entering the northeast doorway. About five minutes later those who had passed before the president began to emerge from the opposite door. I entered the southwest door to witness the form and arrangements for handling such an immense crowd, having been familiar with the long-established custom at the Executive Mansion in Washington. I was in a position to have a full view what was taking place. I was especially attracted by the curved aisle extending diagonally across the floor of the building, the…settees having blue cambric hanging down their backs to make a lane or aisle so that no one could stop. I saw that many of the Park police were stationed along this lane to hasten people out. … Seemingly, thinking a change of form was necessary I was looking directly at the party and noticed Secretary Cortelyou at the rear and back of the receiving party, and who was moving from place to place evidently uneasy."

A picture of McKinley arriving at the Temple of Music

A picture of McKinley greeting people at the Temple of Music minutes before he was shot

Unfortunately, Cortelyou was right to be worried, because not everyone there that day wished him well. In addition to a handful of people who might have disagreed with his politics or disapproved of him personally, there was one man who truly wished him harm. Leon Czolgosz was an anarchist who had come to believe that the only way to improve America was to get rid of the current president. According to one of the doctors who examined him following the assassination, "Czolgosz may be described as a well-nourished, rather good looking, mild-mannered young man with a pleasant facial expression; features, regular; face, smooth-shaven and symmetrical; mouth and ears well-formed and symmetrical; teeth, none missing, but in poor condition from neglect; …hair, light brown and slightly curly; stature, medium — five feet seven and a half inches — and weight — estimated — about 140 pounds. The extremities were in all respects normal. … There were no signs of specific nodes or periosteal tenderness over the usual sites of these lesions, nor was there any evidence upon the head or body of traumatism, excepting a slight deviation of the nose due to a blow which he received at the time of the assassination, and a superficial, perpendicular cicatrix on the left face which he said was the result of a slight injury he received when working in a barbed wire factory. There were no tremors or twitchings of the facial muscles, tongue or hands."

While there was nothing wrong with him physically, Czolgosz's mental state was quite agitated that afternoon. He had decided a few days earlier that he would come to the exposition to kill the president.

As Czolgosz approached McKinley, some nearest him may have noticed that his right hand was wrapped in a handkerchief. This was not unusual at the time since most men carried handkerchiefs, and anyone who saw him may very well have thought he might have cut his hand on something while touring the exposition.

What no one could see was that the handkerchief concealed not a wound but a .32-caliber revolver leaded with five bullets. According to one report published shortly after the shooting, "The man with the bandaged hand and innocent face received no attention from the detectives beyond the mental observation that his right hand was apparently injured, and that he would present his left hand to the president. The President smiled and presented his right hand in a position to meet the left of the approaching man. Hardly a foot of space intervened between the bodies of the two men. Before their hands met two pistol shots rang out, and the president turned slightly to the left and reeled. The bandage on the hand of the tall, innocent looking young man had concealed a revolver. He had fired through the bandage without removing any portion of the handkerchief. … The first bullet entered too high for the purpose of the assassin, who had fired again as soon as his finger could move the trigger. On receiving the first shot President McKinley lifted himself on his toes with something of a gasp. His movement caused the second shot to enter just below the navel. With the second shot the president doubled slightly forward and then sank back. Secret Service Detective Geary caught the president in his arms and President Milburn helped to support him. When the president fell into the arms of Detective Geary he coolly asked: 'Am I shot?' Geary unbuttoned the president's vest, and, seeing blood, replied: 'I fear you are, Mr. President.'"

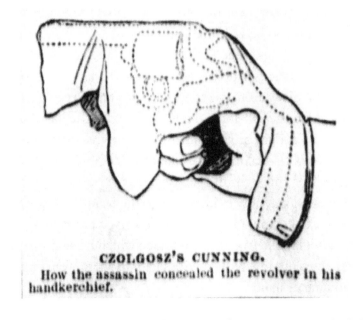

CZOLGOSZ'S CUNNING.
How the assassin concealed the revolver in his handkerchief.

A contemporary illustration of the way Czolgosz concealed the gun

A picture of the spot where McKinley was shot (marked with an X)

Keim was nearby, tragically close to all that happened, and he was also very observant. Accustomed to the political environment, he was unhindered by any sense of awe in his surroundings, and from his vantage point, he observed, "Suddenly hearing two quick, sharp reports, and seeing smoke, I feared that something serious had happened. I saw the president fall back (not fall over) and apparently caught by two persons one on each side. I think Mr. Cortelyou was one. I am not sure about the second one. On the impulse of the moment I rushed forward. In an instant the park guard, stationed along the passageway, seemingly about twenty five feet apart, shouted: 'The President is shot! Put everybody out!' Close the doors! Realizing what had happened, and, observing Secretary Cortelyou and Mr. Millburn and George Foster, of the Secret Service, in attendance, with others, assisting the president, I broke through the improvised aisle…hastily turned around and arranged a settee for the president to rest upon. The President was led forward, along the aisle toward the center of the building walking with great composure, supported by Secretary Cortelyou and Mr. Foster. As he approached the settee, I assisted in placing him upon it. The President sat down with entire self-possession. I began fanning him with my straw hat. Others then began to gather and also fanned him. The President was but slightly pale, and showed little if any signs of nervousness. At this moment the Coast guards and Secret Service men rushed by, carrying the would-be assassin hanging limp in their grasp to the outer entrance to await the patrol wagon. I have since learnt that they took him to a room adjoining the stage."

At first, it was unclear how badly wounded McKinley was. Some hoped that he might have only been grazed, while others feared that his death was imminent. What was clear was that he needed immediate medical care, and an ambulance was sent for at once.

In the meantime, the president was placed in a chair, and according to one report, "His eyes were open and he was clearly conscious of all that had transpired. He looked up into President Milburn s face and gasped: 'Cortelyou,' the name of his private secretary. The President's secretary bent over him. 'Cortelyou,' said the president, 'my wife, be careful about her; don t let her know.' Moved by a paroxysm he writhed to the left and then his eyes fell on the prostrate form of the assassin, Czolgosz, lying on the floor bloody and help less beneath the blows of the guard. The President raised his right hand, red with his own blood, and placed it on the shoulder of his secretary. 'Let no one hurt him,' he gasped, and sank back in the chair, while the guards carried Czolgosz out of his sight."

Keim continued to linger nearby, and though he must have felt some of the same shock that those around him were experiencing, he remembered vivid details of the scene: "The white vest which the president wore had been unbuttoned as well as his shirt front evidently by someone before he was led from the receiving party and showed plainly the powder marks and bullet hole. A little blood had accumulated which attracted the president's eye. It seemed to worry him, somewhat. Secretary Cortelyou, who had now left for a moment to make arrangements for the president's removal, returned. He asked the president: 'Have you much pain?' The President replied, 'No,' turning his head toward the place he had just left and where he had been receiving. Secretary Cortelyou then departed for a second time, and upon returning the president remarked: 'Let no exaggerated reports reach Mrs. McKinley.' (This is exactly as given, all other reports are incorrect.) This he repeated, while Secretary Cortelyou assured him that his wishes would be carried out. In the meantime, occupying a seat on the settee near the president, I kept fanning him so that he might have plenty of fresh air, as did others some five or six in number who had gathered."

Fortunately, the exposition had a field hospital on its grounds, and even an electrically powered ambulance. Though both these items were designed primarily for show, they were fully operational and soon called into use. Keim continued, "Secretary Cortelyou again departed but reappeared when the stretcher arrived with the hospital aids. This was not more than eight minutes after the atrocious deed had been committed and seemed a remarkably quick response to the call, as not more than five minutes has elapsed. Secretary Cortelyou, and I think George Foster, and myself, with the aid of others, assisted the president, who showed the same self-control as all through the terrible ordeal, to the stre[t]cher. He was covered with a blanket by the hospital attendants and willing hands bore him along the aisle to the ambulance, which was waiting at the outer or southwest door. I carried the upper left hand corner, and, having picked up the president's hat from the settee, where he had placed it, and would evidently have been left, I shielded his face from public gaze as we emerged into the light. As we reached the exterior of the building moans and sobs were distinctly heard from the crowd which had gathered and were held back by the police."

A picture of the ambulance

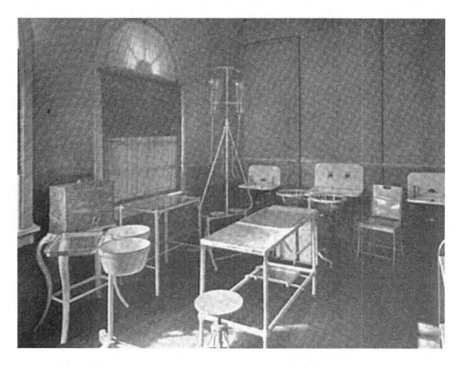

A picture of the operating room in the expo's hospital

As is so often the case when someone famous is injured, there was a great deal of jockeying for position among those who were in charge of caring for him. This was not, to be charitable, primarily a matter of pride but more a matter of each man believing that his leader needed him to be near, and perhaps no man that day felt as responsible for McKinley as Cortelyou. According to Keim, "After the president had been comfortably adjusted in the electric ambulance Secretary Cortelyou desired to ride on the front seat with the driver, but the later objected, not knowing who Mr. Cortelyou was and pushed Mr. Cortelyou off. I said to him (the driver): 'This is the president's secretary and must go!' where upon I pushed Mr. Cortelyou on just as the taller of the attending doctors got up to his seat on the other side evidently because he had not left his seat. This I think now, is the chief service I rendered, for if the ambulance had hurried off Mr. Cortelyou might not have reached the hospital as soon as he did and taken such control of the situation. As the ambulance started, finding no guard on the rear step, I jumped on myself to prevent the door from flying open. There were two hospital attendants on the box with Mr. Cortelyou, and the other riding inside with George Foster. The only government officials accompanying the ambulance were Secretary Cortelyou and myself unless Mr. Foster could be called one. The mounted police, numbering about fifteen, instantly closed in on the rear, and a rapid space was made through the esplanade to the exposition hospital, going north along the west side of the Court of Honor, upon the concrete, and then turned west near the main or west Amherst gate entrance. The smooth concrete payvments [pavement] and the rubber tires ground vibration to a minimum. Many people whom we passed had evidently, as yet, no knowledge of what had transpired within the building."

Dr. Rixey

   Once the party arrived at the hospital, Cortelyou again took the lead. Keim recalled, "Upon halting at the hospital entrance, Secretary Cortelyou was, I think, the first to alight. In the meantime I opened the rear doors, assisted by the young doctor from within the ambulance and George Foster, having been joined by others, the president was borne into the room on the right of the hall, with ample sunlight, and equipped with the most modern surgical appliances. Shortly several surgeons and physicians arrived. Many others on the outside, in vain sought admittance. I think the accompanying doctors told Mr. Cortelyou who was in charge of the Hospital and which city surgeons were of pronounced ability. One or two others came in and I think Dr. Mynter were accepted."

McKinley was taken to the onsite hospital, where he was immediately surrounded by doctors called in following the shooting. Surgery was still in its early stages, but these men were well-trained, particularly in the treatment of bullet wounds. After a brief but intense conversation, they agreed that surgery was called for, and soon, primarily so they could ascertain the extent of the injuries and whether or not the stomach's contents had entered and thus contaminated the abdominal cavity. Keim explained, "In about fifteen minutes, the time being about 4:45 p.m., Dr. Mann arrived. A hurried examination of the president's wound was made, followed by a consultation in the hall, at which an immediate operation was determined upon. Dr. Mann, who came out into the hall told Mr. Cortelyou (in my hearing),'I think we better operate at once' (these are the very words used), to which Secretary Cortelyou assented. Dr. Park came when the operation had progressed about 20 minutes and Dr. Mann explained what he had determined upon and done thus far. While the doctors were washing up preparatory to the trying operation several telegrams were handed in the side or rear windows and I saw the maid take them asking for Mr. Cortelyou, 'who is Mr. Cortelyou?' &c. I seized them and hurriedly went to Mr. Cortelyou, who, after reading them said to me 'I'll not answer any of them now.' In the meantime, at Secretary Cortelyou's request, I stationed myself at one of the doors of the operating room, with George Foster at the other, with instructions not to permit any undesirable persons to pass. Shortly Mr. Foster retired leaving me the only doorkeeper. In the meantime, by the rear entrance to the hospital, several physicians had entered and were pressing their claims. This entrance was quickly barred and several policemen were stationed there with instructions which I gave. During these moments of waiting, the president, while resting on the operating table was heard to say: 'Thy will be done; thy kingdom come', evidently a sentence from the Lord's prayer, and was, I thought, his prayer at the moment. Other broken words followed. I believe he also said: 'God forgive him - he little knew what he was doing.'"

Keim knew little of the details of the surgery, but he was very familiar with the surgical center: "The operating room was most wonderfully provided with modern appliances, and very timely there was scarcely anything lacking: the glass water jars [interpolation illegible], the glass side boards, the excellent planned two west windows letting in the warm setting sun, light and ventilation, the glass trays with instruments lying in solution of antiseptics, the many kinds of antiseptic bandages, the nurses constantly flying in and out bringing what was required without noise and seemingly without instructions all went to show the thoroughness with which this hospital was fitted."

Later, more details of the surgery itself would come out. According to a contemporary report, "The operation lasted almost an hour. A cut about five inches long was made. It was found necessary to turn up the stomach of the president in order to trace the course of the bullet. The bullet s opening in the front wall of the stomach was small and it was carefully closed with sutures, after which a search was made for the hole in the back wall of the stomach. This hole, where the bullet went out of the stomach, was larger than the hole in the front wall of the stomach; in fact, it was a wound over an inch in diameter, jagged and ragged. It was sewed up in three layers. This wound was larger than the wound where the bullet entered the stomach, because the bullet, in its course, forced tissues through ahead of it. In turning up the stomach, an act that was absolutely necessary, and was performed by Dr. Mann with rare skill, the danger was that some of the contents of the stomach might go into the abdominal cavity, and as a result cause peritonitis. It so happened that there was little in the presidents' stomach at the time of the operation. Moreover, subsequent developments tended to show that this feature of the operation was successful and that none of the contents of the stomach entered the abdominal cavity. If any of the contents had entered the cavity the probability is that peritonitis would have set in."

While the doctors were operating, the men outside the surgical room were busy organizing the affairs of the nation. Congress was informed of what had happened, and word of the shooting spread like wildfire through Buffalo, but it was still considered imperative that Ida McKinley be kept in the dark until there was some real news to report, so someone was dispatched to the Milburn home to make sure no one brought her news until after the surgery was over. Keim wrote, "During the operation Secretary Cortelyou was in and out of the room observing the progress of the operation receiving numerous telegrams from all parts of the world and answering urgent calls at the main entrance. Throughout he was as cool and collected as if in the ordinary transaction of business in his office at Washington. His coolness under the terrible strain of the situation was the admiration of all. It allayed undue haste or excitement, and at the same time no moments were lost in indecision. It was undoubtedly due to his extraordinary presence of mind that the president's sufferings were reduced to a minimum. … Before the operation George Foster showed the first or stray bullet, and I wondered as I examined it, how so little a missal [missile] could do so much harm as it seemed to have done. It was an ordinary 32 calibre lead bullet uninjured. As darkness drew on the doctors called for more light. So the overhead electric cluster was turned on, later they asked for a movable light. One was produced and I handed it to Dr. Rixey who held it in as required by the surgeons. As the president's clothes were removed before the operation by the regular attendants, Mr. Foster took charge of them and carried them to the front office, where they were locked up. In the meantime, I had charge of the president's hat, but soon afterwords [sic] placed it with the other articles under Mr. Foster's care. At the close of the operation Dr. Parker said 'Gentlemen before we depart I want to say one thing – let nothing that has been seen or heard in this room be repeated.'"

Although the exposition hospital had an operating theater, it had no place for the patient to recover, so once they thought it was safe, McKinley's doctors loaded the president back into the ambulance and had him driven, very carefully, to Milburn's home. There, they placed him in a comfortable bed and then contacted his wife, who seemed to process the news stoically, though she could not bring herself to write that her husband had been shot by an anarchist. She jotted down in her diary, "Went to Niagra [sic] Falls this morning. My Dearest was receiving in a public hall on our return, when he was shot by a ...."

Around the same time, the public was informed after a bulletin was sent out by the doctors concerning McKinley's condition. Keim noted, "At 7:15 P.M. the president was returned to the electric ambulance assisted by the same willing hands and in about the same order and slowly conveyed by way of the Lincoln Park gate to the Milburn house. As the sad procession was about to leave the grounds, the evening illumination all over the building and grounds began to appear slowly at first, but in about thirty seconds and before they were turned on full head, however, the lights were turned off, leaving the exposition in utter darkness. A very appropriate mark of respect. This was very remarkable for it happened just about the Lincoln gate. As others were leaving the hospital, I was tendered a seat in the carriage of Mr. Goodrich, one of the directors of the exposition who had with him his daughter, and later we were found by Dr. Mynter. We reached the residence immediately after Dr. Rixey and the nurses, having passed the ambulance just outside of the Lincoln gate. The President was very quickly and quietly borne into the mansion and up the stairway to the apartment which had been prepared for him. Just before the party reached the Milburn house steps some hesitancy was apparent which end should go up first. Dr. Mann said the head last so it was done. I soon saw that height was needed at the rear or head so assisted them on up the winding stairs around a dangerous turn to the rear bed room where the president was carefully placed in bed. The stretcher as it was removed from the patient showed clearly the blood stains from the operation, having been used from the first till this moment. In about five minutes all the arrangements had been carried out and the president was resting comfortably as could be expected. I assisted in arranging some furniture that was crowding the room and at the same time cleared the windows so that more air could enter."

Finally, all was in place and there was nothing more to be done that night, certainly not by any non-medical personnel, so most of the bystanders prepared to leave. In fact, due to her own delicate health, Ida McKinley was allowed to sit with her husband by his bedside for only a short period each day. Keim concluded his narrative by recording the last time he saw the president: "I was the last to leave the room, Dr. Mann leaving but a few moments before. The two hospital nurses were in the room when we entered and were most attentive, and together with myself were the only persons there when Dr. Rixey reappeared and for the first time seemed to take charge. The President, but a few moments before, seemed to be coming out from under the influence of ether and was moaning continually, evidently being in much pain. He talked and said many broken words which seemed to connect with those expressed by him before going under the influence of the ether. The surgeons, ambulance corps and friends who had assisted through these trying scenes now departed one by one, leaving Secretary Cortelyou, the medical staff, the stewards and stenographers from the White House who were there to care for the nation's sufferer. This was, I judge, about 8 o'clock. The quiet, sad but cool evening I shall never forget. I bade Mr. Cortelyou goodnight having asked him if there was anything more I could do. I was the last of the assistants to leave and regretted that I could do nothing more for the president we all loved so much."

After the surgery, McKinley spent hour after hour in bed drifting in and out of consciousness, but the doctors believed he was making progress. Indeed, the third day after his operation,

McKinley was alert enough to talk, and he immediately asked about Ida's health. Things looked so promising that Vice President Theodore Roosevelt was assured that he need not cancel his planned hunting trip, so he left for Adirondack Mountains. Dr. McBurney observed, "The fact that there is no unfavorable symptom is a most favorable sign. What we are all waiting for is the lapse of time without the occurrence of inflammation or septic conditions. I want to say right here that in my opinion everything has been done for him that could and should have been done. The case has been most handsomely handled. If he lives he will owe his life to the promptness and skill of the physicians here. The question of time is of the greatest importance in case of this kind. An operation could not have been performed too soon. It was performed in one of the quickest times on record. It will be famous in the history of surgery."

Roosevelt

By Tuesday, September 10, doctors began to discuss when McKinley would be able to take some simple nourishment. In the days before intravenous feedings, it was imperative that a recovering patient eat and drink something to avoid dying of malnutrition or dehydration.

That same night, the doctors in charge of caring for McKinley issued a longer than usual bulletin assuring the public of his continuing improvement: "The condition of the president is unchanged in all important particulars His temperature is 100.6, pulse 114, respiration 28. When the operation was done on Friday last it was noted that the bullet had carried with it a short distance beneath the skin a fragment of the president s coat. This foreign material was, of course, removed, but a slight irritation of the tissues was produced, the evidence of which has appeared only to-night. It has been necessary on account of this slight disturbance to remove a few stitches and partially open the skin wound. This incident cannot give rise to other complications, but it is communicated to the public, as the surgeons in attendance wish to make their bulletins entirely frank. In consequence of this separation of the edges of the surface wound the healing of the same will be somewhat delayed. The President is now well enough to begin to take nourishment by the mouth in the form of pure beef juice."

On Wednesday, September 11, McKinley was allowed his first non-family visitors. Not only did he speak briefly with a number of Congressional representatives, he also continued to keep the broth he was given down.

SENATOR MARK HANNA

THE PRESIDENT'S STEADFAST FRIEND, HASTENING TO HIS SIDE AFTER THE SHOOTING.
ALIGHTING AT THE MILBURN MANSION.

A picture of Senator Hanna arriving at the Milburn house to visit McKinley

However, on Thursday, McKinley took a sudden turn for the worse; his heart was beating too fast and unevenly, owing perhaps to the strain placed on his system by having to digest the broth. After rallying briefly, his heart began to slow, and word was sent to family members and others close to McKinley that they should come to Buffalo as quickly as possible. Vice President Roosevelt was also informed of McKinley's condition and advised to head to Buffalo.

At about 2:00 a.m. on Friday morning, September 13, McKinley's heart slowed to a dangerous level, so doctors injected him with a number of drugs in the hopes of strengthening it. Again, McKinley rallied, but this time only slightly. In fact, the gangrene that had begun to form in his abdomen within seconds of the shooting had taken full hold of him and he was beginning to experience massive organ failure.

By Friday evening, it was apparent that McKinley was dying, and he told the doctors, "It is useless, gentlemen. I think we ought to have prayer." Later, he told his sobbing wife, "We are all going, we are all going. God's will be done, not ours." The couple then shared a final moment softly singing McKinley's favorite hymn, "Nearer, My God, to Thee." At 8:30 p.m., the doctors issued the following statement: "The President's condition this evening is not quite so good. His food has not agreed with him and has been stopped. Excretion has not yet been properly established. The kidneys are acting well. His pulse is not satisfactory, but has improved in the last two hours. The wound is doing well. He is resting quietly. Temperature, 100.2; pulse, 128."

Less than 6 hours later, McKinley died at 2:15 a.m. on Saturday, September 14, 1901.

The Aftermath of McKinley's Death

McKinley's funeral train in Buffalo

In one of the greatest ironies of American history, President McKinley was succeeded by Roosevelt because of the machinations by people who wanted to remove Roosevelt from power in New York. Now, instead of being consigned into a political abyss, Roosevelt was now the most powerful person in the United States.

In the wake of McKinley's death, Roosevelt informed the American people of what had happened and announced when McKinley's funeral would be held: "A terrible bereavement has befallen our people. The President of the United States has been struck down; a crime not only against the Chief Magistrate, but against every law-abiding and liberty-loving citizen. President McKinley crowned a life of largest love for his fellow men, of earnest endeavor for their welfare, by a death of Christian fortitude; and both the way in which he lived his life and the way in which, in the supreme hour of trial, he met his death will remain forever a precious heritage of our people. It is meet that we as a nation express our abiding love and reverence for his life, our deep sorrow for his untimely death. Now, Therefore, I, Theodore Roosevelt, President of the United States of America, do appoint Thursday next, September 19, the day in which the body of the dead President will be laid in its last earthly resting place, as a day of mourning and prayer throughout the United States. I earnestly recommend all the people to assemble on that day in their respective places of divine worship, there to bow down in submission to the will of Almighty God, and to pay out of full hearts the homage of love and reverence to the memory of the great and good President, whose death has so sorely smitten the nation."

Pictures of McKinley's state funeral back in Washington

All the while, as people focused their attention on the wounded president, the police and Secret Service had other concerns. They hauled Czolgosz to a local jail for questioning but did not have any difficulty getting a confession from him. When he was asked why he wanted to kill the president, he apparently replied, "I am an Anarchist. I am a disciple of Emma Goldman. Her words set me on fire. I deny that I have had an accomplice at any time. I don t regret my act, because I was doing what I could for the great cause. I am not connected with the Paterson group or with those Anarchists who sent Bresci to Italy to kill Humbert. I had no confidants; no one to help me. I was alone absolutely." Before the day was over, he had written and signed a statement declaring, "I was born in Detroit nearly twenty-nine years ago. My parents were Russian Poles. They came here forty-two years ago. I got my education in the public schools of Detroit and then went to Cleveland, where I got work. In Cleveland I read books on socialism and met a great many Socialists. I was pretty well known as a Socialist in the West. After being in Cleveland for several years I went to Chicago, where I remained seven months, after which I went to Newburg, on the outskirt of Cleveland, and went to work in the Newburg wire mills. During the last five years I have had as friends Anarchists in Chicago, Cleveland, Detroit, and other Western cities, and I suppose I became more or less bitter. Yes, I know I was bitter. I never had much luck at anything and this preyed upon me. It made me morose and envious, but what started the craze to kill was a lecture I heard some little time ago by Emma Goldman. She was in Cleveland and I and other Anarchists went to hear her. She set me on fire. Her doctrine that all rulers should be exterminated was what set me to thinking so that my head nearly split with the pain. Miss Goldman's words went right through me and when I left the lecture I had made up my mind that I would have to do something heroic for the cause I loved."

Goldman

Czolgosz in jail

For his part, Czolgosz claimed that while Goldman's words were inspiration, he had planned the assassination by September 3. In fact, some believe that he had considered acting earlier by following McKinley when he took walks near his home in Canton, Ohio, but either way, the assassin admitted to police, "Eight days ago, while I was in Chicago, I read in a Chicago newspaper of President McKinley's visit to the Pan-American Exposition at Buffalo. That day I bought a ticket for Buffalo and got there with the determination to do something, but I did not know just what. I thought of shooting the president, but I had not formed a plan. I went to live at 1078 Broadway, which is a saloon and hotel. John Nowak, a Pole, a sort of politician who has led his people here for years, owns it. I told Nowak that I came to see the fair. He knew nothing about what was setting me crazy. I went to the Exposition grounds a couple of times a day. Not until Tuesday morning did the resolution to shoot the president take a hold of me. It was in my heart; there was no escape for me. I could not have conquered it had my life been at stake. There were thousands of people in town on Tuesday. I heard it was President's Day. All these people seemed bowing to the great ruler. I made up my mind to kill that ruler. I bought a 32-caliber revolver and loaded it."

The twists and turns of history can be strange, and for whatever reason, fate intervened and Czolgosz did not shoot McKinley on that Tuesday. Instead, as he explained, "On Tuesday night I went to the Fair grounds and was near the railroad gate when the presidential party arrived. I tried to get near him, but the police forced me back. They forced everybody back so that the great ruler could pass. I was close to the president when he got into the grounds, but was afraid to attempt the assassination because there were so many men in the bodyguard that watched him. I was not afraid of them or that I should get hurt, but afraid I might be seized and that my chance would be gone forever. Well, he went away that time and I went home. On Wednesday I went to the grounds and stood right near the president, right under him near the stand from which he spoke. I thought half a dozen times of shooting while he was speaking, but I could not get close enough. I was afraid I might miss, and then the great crowd was always jostling, and I was afraid lest my aim fail. I waited on Wednesday, and the president got into his carriage again, and a lot of men were about him and formed a cordon that I could not get through. I was tossed about by the crowd, and my spirits were getting pretty low. I was almost hopeless that night as I went home."

Had Czolgosz's missed opportunities changed his mind, there's no telling how differently things may have gone for the nation, but he remained determined. "Yesterday morning I went again to the Exposition grounds. Emma Goldman's speech was still burning me up. I waited near the central entrance for the president, who was to board his special train from that gate, but the police allowed nobody but the president's party to pass where the train waited, so I stayed at the grounds all day waiting. During yesterday I first thought of hiding my pistol under my handkerchief. I was afraid if I had to draw, it from my pocket I would be seen and seized by the guards. I got to the Temple of Music the first one and waited at the spot where the reception was to be held. Then he came, the president the ruler and I got in line and trembled and trembled until I got right up to him, and then I shot him twice, through my white handkerchief. I would have fired more, but I was stunned by a blow in the face a frightful blow that knocked me down and then everybody jumped on me. I thought I would be killed and was surprised the way they treated me."

Czolgosz's decision to murder McKinley is truly ironic considering that just a few days earlier, *The Free Society Newspaper* accused him of being an anti-anarchist spy. It seems that in his enthusiasm, he had been asking too many questions about what anarchism was, where one could find a meeting of anarchists, and who the local leaders were. The *Free Society* had warned, "ATTENTION! The attention of the comrades is called to another spy. He is well dressed, of medium height, rather narrow shoulders, blond and about 25 years of age. Up to the present he has made his appearance in Chicago and Cleveland. In the former place he remained but a short time, while in Cleveland he disappeared when the comrades had confirmed themselves of his identity and were on the point of exposing him. His demeanor is of the usual sort, pretending to be greatly interested in the cause, asking for names or soliciting aid for acts of contemplated violence. If this same individual makes his appearance elsewhere the comrades are warned in advance, and can act accordingly."

Born in Russia in the late 19th century, Emma Goldman had come to the United States as a teen and quickly grew attracted to anarchy and socialism over what she viewed as unfair class structures in her new home, especially in the wake of the Haymarket riots. But while many simply grumbled about the Gilded Age in private or denounced it in print, Goldman was a woman of action, from being involved in the attempted assassination of tycoon Henry Clay Frick to publishing anarchist journals and passing around information about contraception.

As a result, Goldman was already notorious before McKinley's death, and when Czolgosz mentioned her by name, it had obvious ramifications for her as well. Indeed, as soon as the authorities learned that Czolgosz had been influenced in his plan by Goldman, they immediately saw an opportunity to arrest her, for they had long been concerned about her anti-American activities and were looking for an excuse to take her into custody. Of course, it did not help that she had spoken out about the case and told a reporter, "The boy in Buffalo is a creature at bay. Millions of people are ready to spring on him and tear him limb from limb. He committed the act for no personal reasons or gain. He did it for what is his ideal: the good of the people. That is why my sympathies are with him. On the other hand, William McKinley, suffering and probably near death, is merely a human being to me now. That is why I would nurse him."

Goldman remembered the moment she learned she had been named by Czolgosz: "I went to the stationery store to see the owner. … While I was waiting for the man to fill out his order, I caught the headline of the newspaper lying on his desk: 'ASSASSIN OF PRESIDENT MCKINLEY AN ANARCHIST, CONFESSES TO HAVING BEEN INCITED BY EMMA GOLDMAN, WOMAN ANARCHIST WANTED.' By great effort I strove to preserve my composure, completed the business, and walked out of the store. At the next corner I bought several papers and went to a restaurant to read them. They were filled with the details of the tragedy, reporting also the police raid of the Isaak house in Chicago and the arrest of everyone found there. The authorities were going to hold the prisoners until Emma Goldman was found, the papers stated. Already two hundred detectives had been sent out throughout the country to track down Emma Goldman. … When I was through with the papers, it became clear to me that I must immediately go to Chicago. The Isaak family, Hippolyte, our old comrade Jay Fox, a most active man in the labour movement, and a number of others were being held without bail until I should be found. It was plainly my duty to surrender myself. I knew there was neither reason nor the least proof to connect me with the shooting. I would go to Chicago."

Once in Chicago, Goldman was indeed arrested and interrogated, but there was no evidence to convict her of anything not covered by her right to free speech, so she was released. Undeterred, she shocked and horrified even her most ardent supporters by publicly defending Czolgosz: "As an anarchist, I am opposed to violence. But if the people want to do away with assassins, they must do away with the conditions which produce murderers."

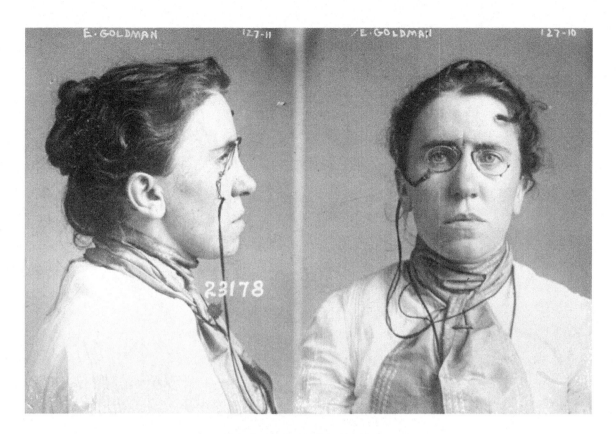

Goldman's 1901 mug shot

The *Chicago Daily Tribune*'s condemnation of Goldman

This stance proved to be very harmful not just to Goldman but to the entire movement, and it brought down the wrath of many across the grieving nation. The new president, Teddy Roosevelt, himself something of a populist, declared, "The anarchist, and especially the anarchist in the United States, is merely one type of criminal, more dangerous than any other because he represents the same depravity in a greater degree. The man who advocates anarchy directly or indirectly, in any shape or fashion, or the man who apologizes for anarchists and their deeds, makes himself morally accessory to murder before the fact. The anarchist is a criminal whose perverted instincts lead him to prefer confusion and chaos to the most beneficent form of social order. His protest of concern for workingmen is outrageous in its impudent falsity; for if the political institutions of this country do not afford opportunity to every honest and intelligent son of toil, then the door of hope is forever closed against him. The anarchist is everywhere not merely the enemy of system and of progress, but the deadly foe of liberty. If ever anarchy is triumphant, its triumph will last for but one red moment, to be succeeded, for ages by the gloomy night of despotism."

As Goldman herself noted, "After the death of McKinley the campaign against anarchism and its adherents continued with increased venom. The press, the pulpit, and other public mouthpieces were frantically vying with each other in their fury against the common enemy. ... Anti-anarchist bills followed each other in quick succession, their congressional sponsors busy inventing new methods for the extermination of anarchists. Senator Hawley evidently did not consider his professional wisdom sufficient to slay the anarchist dragon. He declared publicly that he would give a thousand dollars to get a shot at an anarchist. It was a cheap offer considering the price Czolgosz had paid for his shot."

On September 13, as McKinley lay dying, Czolgosz was transferred from the police headquarters where he had been held since the shooting to the Erie County Women's Penitentiary. While he was there, he was apparently a model prisoner, cooperative and pleasant to the guards, whom he seemed to view not as his captors but as fellow victims of the system of government under which Americans were laboring.

Three days later, he was brought before County Judge Emery for arraignment. After the Grand Jury indicted him for murder, he was transferred to Auburn State Prison. The indictment read, in part:

> "That the said Leon F. Czolgosz, ... with force and arms in and upon one William McKinley...being, willfully, feloniously and from a deliberate and premeditated design to effect the death of said William McKinley, did make an assault, and the said Leon F. Czolgosz, alias Fred Nieman, then and there willfully, feloniously and from a deliberate and premeditated design to effect the death of the said William McKinley, did shoot off and discharge to, at, against and upon the said William McKinley a certain pistol and firearm, then and there charged and loaded with gunpowder and leaden bullets, ...shot out of the pistol and firearm...in and upon the stomach, abdomen and body of the said William McKinley, one mortal wound...the said William McKinley...until the fourteenth day of September...did languish, and, languishing, did live, on which said last-mentioned day he...of the said mortal wound, did die; contrary to the form of the statute in such case made

and provided, and against the peace of the people of the State of New York and their dignity.

(Signed.) THOMAS PENNEY, District Attorney of Erie County."

Apparently, Neiman was an Americanized version of his mother's maiden name, and he sometimes used the alias Fred Nieman when he was trying to hide what he was doing.

Fittingly, the arraignment itself proved to be something a mystery to many people, as Czolgosz refused to speak out on his own behalf or even allow his lawyers to do so. Meanwhile, Everett gave a moving description of the event:

"'Are you guilty, or not guilty?' was the question which the Law asked of him.

He was placed with hands unbound in the presence of a sedate tribunal of one of the tribunals which all the organs of his reed had been maligning in their every issue; and there he was asked:

'Are you guilty, or not guilty?'

District Attorney Penney almost shouted the words at Leon Czolgosz, sitting in the county courtroom at 3 o clock this afternoon. The assassin did not even turn his eyes toward his questioner.

'Are you guilty? Answer yes or no!' thundered the district attorney, but the fair-haired monster in the chair paid no heed.

'Do you understand what has been read?' asked Mr. Penney.

…The assassin leaned forward in his chair, then dropped his eyes, then leaned back in silence.

'You have been indicted for murder in the first degree,' said Mr. Penney.

…Judge Loren L. Lewis, former justice of the Supreme Court, who had been assigned to the defense of the assassin by Judge Edward K. Emery, then arose and addressed the court. It was at once apparent that the duty was distasteful, but Mr. Lewis entered a plea of 'Not Guilty.'"

After he entered the plea, Lewis went on to explain to the court his awkward situation; while Czolgosz would happily speak with all those around him, he would have nothing to do with his court-appointed attorneys. Everett noted, "Attorney Lewis then told the court that he had called upon the prisoner, but had been met with a stubborn refusal to discuss the case. Czolgosz would not even admit that he wished the services of counsel. Mr. Lewis asked the court for permission to introduce alienists to examine into the prisoner's mental condition, as this step had already been taken by the attorneys for the people. He mentioned incidentally that he was sorry his name had been connected with the case, but that as a lawyer and an officer of the court he felt himself obligated to carry out its wishes. ... Mr. Lewis request to be permitted to introduce alienists gave rise to the prevalent belief that the defense will be built upon the theory of insanity."

It seems likely Czolgosz shunned his attorneys because, at least to him, they represented the establishment and the government, but regardless, since he would not speak to them, his lawyers, Lewis and Judge R. C. Titus, simply went with a plea of insanity. Of course, the prosecution was able to show without a doubt that Czolgosz definitely pulled the trigger, so there could be no doubt about that. With little strategy available to him, Lewis admitted Czolgosz's guilt but insisted that "the only question that can be discussed or considered in this case is ... whether that act was that of a sane person. If it was, then the defendant is guilty of the murder ... If it was the act of an insane man, then he is not guilty of murder but should be acquitted of that charge and would then be confined in a lunatic asylum."

In an article published in *The Journal of Mental Pathology* in January 1902, Dr. Carlos McDonald, who had examined Czolgosz while he was in prison, observed, "In view of the great importance of the case, it is regrettable that no experts were called to testify on the trial as to the prisoner's mental condition, in order that it might appear on the record of the trial that his mental state was inquired into and determined by competent authority. Had the experts on either side been given the opportunity of thus stating officially their unanimous conclusion, together with the grounds on which it was based and the methods by which it was reached, it would have left in the public mind no room for reasonable doubt as to its absolute correctness, and that it had been arrived at only by the rules of professional conduct governing the examination of such cases."

Still, McDonald recognized that the defense was indeed doing the best it could under the parameters that Czolgosz himself had set. After all, it was very difficult to defend a man who seemed to have no desire to be acquitted. McDonald recalled, "On Thursday, September 19th, 1901, I received a telegram requesting me to meet Mr. Adelbert Moot, President of the Erie County Bar Association, in Buffalo, New York, on the following morning. On my arrival in Buffalo the next day, Mr. Moot informed me that he had sent for me for the purpose of requesting me to inquire into the mental condition of Leon F. Czolgosz...whose trial was to begin on the following Monday. Mr. Moot further stated in substance that three local experts had already examined the prisoner for the District Attorney, but in view of the enormity of the offense and the fact that there obviously could be no legitimate defense other than insanity, it was deemed important, in the interests of justice, that his mental condition should be investigated by other experts acting in behalf of the defense, or at least independently of the prosecution to the end that the prisoner should be accorded every legal right, there being no desire to convict him if he were not mentally responsible, and that I had been selected for this responsible duty."

McDonald seemed convinced that in spite of the nation's demand for swift and fierce justice, there was nothing rigged about the trial, and that the state seemed committed to giving Czolgosz as fair a trial as the circumstances allowed. He continued, "With a deep sense of the responsibility involved, I consented to act, provided it should be distinctly understood that I was not there as a partisan expert in behalf of either side, but simply in a professional capacity to aid in determining the real mental state of the prisoner, and providing further that my selection would be acceptable to the eminent counsel whom the Bar Association had selected for the defense, should they decide to accept that duty, a matter which was then undecided. On the following morning — Saturday — Mr. Moot informed me that the gentlemen referred to had consented to act…. They also assented readily to my proposal to invite Dr. Arthur W. Hurd to become associated with me professionally in the case…. Being unable to establish communication with Dr. Hurd before evening of that day, and in view of the short time intervening before the trial, I decided to make a preliminary examination of Czolgosz alone, and did so that afternoon, in the District Attorney's office, first disclosing to him my identity and the object of my interview, and informing him of his legal right to decline to answer any question I might ask him."

McDonald ultimately concluded that the defense's basis for its insanity plea was pretty weak. "I examined him again on the following day — Sunday — in the jail, jointly with Dr. Hurd, and in the presence of one of his guards who was questioned at length, respecting his observations of him in the jail, as to his habits of eating, sleeping, talking, reading, etc. We subsequently interviewed the District Attorney and the Superintendent of Police, General Bull, who gave us all the facts and information in their possession respecting the case. The statement which Czolgosz made to the District Attorney shortly after his arrest, throws much light on his mental condition on the day of the crime, but that official deemed it his duty to refuse to allow me to publish it. We also conferred at length with the people's experts — Drs. Fowler, Crego and Putnam, who stated to us separately and in detail their observations and examinations of him. We also observed him carefully in the court room throughout the trial. After our examination of Czolgosz, on Sunday, we reached the conclusion, independently of each other, that he was sane, and we so informed his counsel, on Monday morning before the trial began. It should be said that owing to the limited time — two days — at our disposal prior to the trial and the fact that his family relatives resided in a distant state and were not accessible for interrogation, we were unable to obtain a history of his heredity, beyond what he himself gave us."

On the other hand, the prosecutor was able to make much of Czolgosz's obsession with anarchism and paint him as a man who knew perfectly well what he was doing and what the consequences were likely to be when he killed the president. Then, to top everything off, White sent the jury off with pretty clear instructions to ignore any claims that Czolgosz was mentally unbalanced. According to McDonald, "The jury retired for deliberation about 4 p. m., and returned in less than half an hour with a verdict of guilty of murder in the first degree. Czolgosz heard the verdict of the jury standing, and without appreciable display of emotion. Several of the jurors were reported to have said after the trial, that the jury was in favor of conviction unanimously from the first, and could have rendered a verdict without leaving their seats, but deemed it best to make a pretense at deliberation 'for appearance' sake.' Czolgosz was remanded to jail for two days, and on Thursday, September 26th, was sentenced to be executed by electricity at Auburn Prison, in the week beginning October 28th, 1901. When Czolgosz returned to his cell after his conviction he ate a hearty supper, and soon thereafter went to bed and slept continuously until midnight, when the guard was changed, when he awoke for a few minutes, and then slept again until 6 a. m., when he arose and took a short walk in the cell corridor, after which he made a careful toilet, and at 7.30 partook of a hearty breakfast. He talked freely, as usual, on ordinary topics, but maintained his usual silence respecting his crime, and would not talk of the trial or the verdict. On Thursday, September 26th, he was removed from the Buffalo jail to the State Prison at Auburn, N. Y., where he was confined in a 'death cell,' until his execution took place."

On October 29, 1901, less than two months after he shot McKinley, Czolgosz was scheduled to be executed at Auburn Prison. This was swift justice even by the standards of that era, but he put up no resistance and made no legal appeals. Charles Huntley witnessed the execution and subsequently described it: "Czolgosz did not show any signs of fear and he did not tremble or turn pale; he walked into the death room between two men, and walked with a firm step. He stumbled as he came into the room but did not fall, nor did his knees weaken. I was quite surprised at his demeanor, as was everyone else, I should say. He was perfectly strong and calm. He just slid himself into the chair exactly as a man might who expected to enjoy a half hour's repose. The fact that in a moment a death current was to be forced through him did not seem to perturb him in the least. … He spoke very plainly and in a voice which did not waver in the slightest degree. He said first that he was not sorry for having killed the president, and, as the straps which bound his jaws were put in place, he said that he was sorry he could not see his father. … It was a general surprise to hear his voice after the men had begun to affix the electrodes. The witnesses were somewhat startled and were amazed at the man's calmness. We all kept our eyes on him and listened most attentively. But the men at work beside him and in front, of him did not pause. They kept on affixing the appliances. Evidently Czolgosz had prepared something to say and what he said was part of his prepared piece. … I wouldn't say that he tried to make a hero of himself. There was no spirit of bravado manifest at all. He said a few things just as if he felt it his duty to say them."

Apparently Czolgosz's last words were, "I killed the president because he was the enemy of the good people – the good working people. I am not sorry for my crime." However, some who were listening thought that, at the very last minute, he said softly, as if fighting his emotion, "I am only sorry I could not get to see my father."

Sheriff Samuel Caldwell, who was present at the execution, reported, "I was impressed with the idea that the assassin was a man of great nerve. Although guards had hold of his arms, the prisoner could have walked unaided to the chair. Aside from the prisoner's last words, there was not a sound in the death chamber, and the prisoner himself gave no evidence of fear. As soon as he had been seated in the chair and his face covered so that his nose and mouth were alone exposed, Warden Mead raised his hand and Electrician Davis turned on the current which snuffed out the prisoner's life as with a snap of the finger. The electrician then felt the prisoner's jugular vein. Dr. MacDonald did the same, and was followed by Prison Physician Gerin. The doctors then stepped back, and Warden Mead again raised his hand. Again the current was applied and was continued about 50 seconds. When the electricity was again shut off, the physicians examined the body by the usual means, and at the end pronounced that the man was dead. The witnesses left the death chamber before the body was removed to the operating table in the autopsy room. I signed the document. swearing that I saw the electrocution of the assassin. The doctors remained for the autopsy, but I came home immediately. The prisoner's nerve was evidenced by his conduct from the moment he entered the death chamber. No groan escaped him, and his lips did not even move except when he was making his final statement to the effect that he did not repent his crime. When the electricity entered the assassin's body it stiffened with successive jerks, but death was so quick that he did not have time to groan."

In keeping with the practice of the day, Czolgosz was given three jolts of 1800 volts each, and the physicians on hand pronounced him dead at 7:14. His brother, Waldek, and his brother-in-law, Frank Bandowski, were present to witness the execution and afterward approached the warden and asked to have Czolgosz's body to take home for burial. However, the warden would not allow it and told them they "would never be able to take it away" without being mobbed by the crowds gathered outside. Instead, Czolgosz's body was taken back into custody and turned over to Edward Spitzka for autopsy.

DR. EDWARD ANTHONY SPITZKA
Director and Professor of General Anatomy
The Daniel Bangle Institute of Anatomy of
the Jefferson Medical College
Philadelphia, Pa.

Spitzka

In answering some of the lingering questions concerning Czolgosz's mental state, Spitzka could only say, "It is a probable fact that certain classical aberrations from the normal standard of brain structure are commonly encountered in some criminals and degraded classes of society; and some workers who have attempted to found a school of degeneracy have endeavored to explain the manifestation of crime and other psychic abnormalities by the fact of 'accidental persistence of lower types of human organization.' But these structural anomalies, so far as they have been described in the brains of criminals, are too few and too insufficiently corroborated to warrant us in drawing conclusions from them. Various perversions or anomalies of mind may exist in this class without presenting a uniform criminal type from the anatomical aspect. Of course, it is far more difficult, — and it is impossible in some cases — to establish sanity upon the results of an examination of the brain, than it is to prove insanity. This difficulty is so much the more complex because some forms of psychoses have absolutely no ascertainable anatomical basis. The assumption has been made that these psychoses depend rather on circulatory and bio-chemical disturbances. So far as this question touches upon the brain and body of Czolgosz, there have been found absolutely none of those conditions of any of the viscera that could have been at the bottom of any mental derangement. Taking all in all, the verdict must be, 'socially diseased and perverted, but not mentally diseased.' The most horrible violations of human law cannot always be condoned by the plea of insanity. 'The wild beast slumbers in us all. It is not always necessary to invoke insanity to explain its awakening.'"

Following the autopsy, Czolgosz's body was buried in the prison cemetery, with acid having been doused on it to speed up decomposition. Most of his belongings were burned, but the gun he used in his heinous act was kept and is now part of collection of the Buffalo History Museum.

Though he would obviously not live to see it or comprehend it, Czolgosz's assassination of McKinley may have had a bigger impact on history than any other president's assassin other than John Wilkes Booth. Even without diving into his life and career, the fact that Theodore Roosevelt is on Mount Rushmore alongside George Washington, Thomas Jefferson, and Abraham Lincoln says volumes about his place in American history. That alone makes clear Roosevelt is among the nation's most influential and important Presidents.

Thanks to the death of McKinley, Roosevelt had the opportunity to mold the presidency in crucial ways. Roosevelt was able to create the "bully pulpit" of the presidency and ensure that he set the nation's legislative agenda by giving press statements regularly. Every president has since used the office to attempt to determine the nation's legislative priorities.

This personal strengthening of the presidency spilled over into an administrative augmentation of the office of President. Though the Sherman Anti Trust Act had been passed in the 1880s, all presidents before Roosevelt underutilized its power. Roosevelt consolidated much of the power delegated to him by Congress and ensured that the president took an active role in administering the government of the United States. He also expanded the presidential cabinet and created many new administrative departments, widening the breadth of the nation's federal bureaucracy. Only his fifth cousin, Franklin, would outshine him in this pursuit decades later.

On domestic policy, Theodore Roosevelt's presidency was the height of American progressivism, again outshone only by his distant cousin decades later. Roosevelt brought the ideology of limited, free-market government to its heels and instituted numerous reforms geared towards breaking corporate power and aiding consumers.

Roosevelt's presidency is also credited with making America a global player in international relations. The Panama Canal and the Roosevelt Corollary ensured the U.S. would dominate the Western Hemisphere, and the Portsmouth Treaty also expanded the nation's influence in places it had previously never gone. Roosevelt's expansion of the military and support for an interventionist policy was a marked departure from previous administrations; until Roosevelt, the United States had been rigidly isolationist since Washington offered his neutrality advice as President.

Thus, it was Roosevelt who ensured the nation would not merely be an economic powerhouse but also participate actively and powerfully in the international sphere. It can safely be said that Roosevelt opened the doors to what would become the "American Century."

Online Resources

Other 19th century history titles by Charles River Editors

Other titles about William McKinley on Amazon

Bibliography

Armstrong, William H. (2000). Major McKinley: William McKinley and the Civil War. Kent, Ohio: The Kent State University Press.

Gould, Lewis L. (1980). The Presidency of William McKinley. American Presidency. Lawrence, Kansas: University Press of Kansas.

Jones, Stanley L. (1964). The Presidential Election of 1896. Madison, Wisconsin: University of Wisconsin Press.

Leech, Margaret (1959). In the Days of McKinley. New York: Harper and Brothers.

McCullough, David (1977). The Path Between the Seas: The Creation of the Panama Canal 1870–1914. New York: Touchstone.

McElroy, Richard L. (1996). William McKinley and Our America. Canton, Ohio: Stark County Historical Society. ISBN 978-0-9634712-1-5.

McKinley, William (1893). Speeches and Addresses of William McKinley. New York: D. Appleton and Company.

Merry, Robert W. (2017). President McKinley: Architect of the American Century. New York: Simon & Schuster.

Phillips, Kevin (2003). William McKinley. New York: Times Books. I.

Pratt, Walter F. (1999). The Supreme Court under Edward Douglass White, 1910–1921. Columbia, South Carolina: University of South Carolina Press. ISBN 978-1-57003-309-4.

Rove, Karl (2015). The Triumph of William McKinley: Why the Election of 1896 Still Matters. New York: Simon & Schuster.

Williams, R. Hal (2010). Realigning America: McKinley, Bryan and the Remarkable Election of 1896. Lawrence, Kansas: University Press of Kansas.

Free Books by Charles River Editors

We have brand new titles available for free most days of the week. To see which of our titles are currently free, click on this link.

Discounted Books by Charles River Editors

We have titles at a discount price of just 99 cents everyday. To see which of our titles are currently 99 cents, click on this link.

Made in the USA
Coppell, TX
13 August 2020

33027018R00050